Child Development for Day Care Workers

Houghton Mifflin Company · Boston

Atlanta · Dallas · Geneva, Illinois · Hopewell, New Jersey

Palo Alto · London

Child Development for Day Care Workers

Ruth Highberger

University of Tennessee

Carol Schramm

Printed in the U.S.A.
Library of Congress Catalog Card Number: 75-31008
ISBN: 0-395-20631-6

Contents

Preface

This book was written for beginning students, para-professionals, and other day care workers who wish to increase their understanding of infants and children. Although there are many guides for use in day care programs, none of them, to our knowledge, has gathered together basic information on the development of children and suggested the implications of this information for day care programs. In applying this information to day care work, we have drawn on our own experience in directing day care centers and in teaching.

We have attempted to present the information in as simple a way as possible, since our concern is to provide you with basic material upon which you can build your own program. Important terms are defined in the text and listed in a glossary at the end of each chapter, as well as in the comprehensive glossary at the end of the book.

Although it has been our experience that many students dislike learning about theory at the beginning of a course, we believe that theory serves as the foundation for further knowledge and professional growth and we therefore have presented this material in Chapter 1. Though this information may be demanding, we feel that it can easily be adapted to particular classroom situations. For those of you who are interested in further information, a list of supplementary readings is at the end of the chapter.

The emphasis throughout the book is on individuality and the importance of understanding each child in terms of the stage of development he or she is going through. There are chapters on infants, toddlers, and preschool children. These include discussions of the development of each of these stages out of the preceding one. Chapter 7 is devoted to the importance of working closely with parents, and specific suggestions for procedures that may be used are included. Chapter 8 offers suggestions for increasing your information about children, and Chapter 9 is a brief history of programs for infants and young children.

We wish to acknowledge the valuable assistance given to the development of the manuscript, at all stages, by the reviewers, who were Ms. Jeanne Armstrong, Lane Community College (Oregon); Mrs. Marilyn Brock, Los Angeles Harbor College; Mrs. Marian Carlin, Oregon State University; Ms. Tena Carr, Modesto Junior College (California); Ms. Dorothy Sciarra, University of Cincinnati; Ms. Sylvia Skousen, Mesa Community College (Arizona); Mrs. Mary Stroud, Long Beach City College; and Mrs. Jane Teleki, University of Oklahoma.

Ruth Highberger

Carol Schramm

Introduction

This is a book about young children and the way they develop and behave. It is very likely that your interest in day care work results from a concern with children and a desire to work closely with them. Your interest may well have developed from the special appeal that all young creatures have, like kittens, and puppies. Human young are even more appealing because each one is an individual, each one a little different from the other. Realizing this may have increased your wish to become involved with children.

You may also have learned that along with the enjoyment and satisfaction you gain in working with children there goes a great responsibility to them as well. Your influence on a young child can have long-range effects, and it is important that you understand and accept this as a responsibility. This book provides information on how children develop that should help you to do this.

Studying children can be a life-long task. The research already completed, and that which is being done now, is considerable. The fields of anthropology, nutrition, medicine, and others, all contribute to the large and growing body of information. No one person could ever learn all there is to know about children, and no one book could contain all the information. However, as a day care worker, you should have some basic information to be prepared for your work.

No doubt you will be involved in planning the activity program for the children in your care. To plan wisely, you must understand their particular skills and interests. For example, if you know that toddlers (ages one to two and a half) spend their days in constant motion, you won't plan for them to sit still in a story group; story groups work well for five-year-olds, who are far less active. And, when you work with three-year-olds using scissors, you won't expect them to cut out perfect circles and squares, because you will know that at this age children have trouble making scissors cut paper.

Knowledge of child development helps adults observe children more precisely. Good observation is the basis of good teaching, but time for observation of individual children is limited. Knowledge of child development will help you focus on what to expect and on where special attention is needed. Thus, for example, you can focus on the growing vocabulary of a two-year-old and pay less attention to his or her incorrect grammar, which will be corrected later. Knowledge of the children's skills and daily observations will help you to plan a program and select equipment.

Knowing how children develop will also help you to handle your own feelings about the way they behave. You all have memories of the way you were brought up and were expected to behave. Though you are only aware of some of these memories, any of them can influence the way you evaluate a child's behavior. Though you may feel that the way you were brought up is the only "right" way, there are actually many different ways to rear children and many different ways of behaving.

Children in day care centers come from many different kinds of families, and those families have many different ways of behaving. This is important to remember. Many of you were punished and made to feel guilty about behavior such as spitting, biting, and toilet accidents. If you know that this is common for two- and four-year-olds, you can accept these events and keep them in proper perspective. You can also help children develop more acceptable behavior, like expressing anger in words and eliminating in the toilet. In effect, you can help children because you understand why they behave as they do.

In considering their behavior, you must also remember that these children are growing up in a world that is different from the one you knew when you were young. Today's children naturally reflect the great changes that have taken place. And, furthermore, they will grow up into a world which will be still more changed.

In your work, you will also be involved with parents. Professional knowledge about children should be shared with them to help them become better parents. Many parents have unrealistic expectations for a child at a particular stage of development, and many conflicts between parent and child can result from these misunderstandings. Parents may consider their child's behavior unacceptable in some way, but if they know that it is common in children of that age, they will feel better about the child and about themselves too. This added confidence will allow them to help their child's behavior mature. Overall, the child, the parent, and the day care worker will all benefit.

Now you can see how knowledge of the way children develop can influence program planning, observation of children, feelings about children, and work with parents. But this knowledge will not solve every problem.

Over and over again in your work, you will be faced with problems with a particular child at a particular time which you must do something about. What do you do, for example, when four-year-old Jimmy throws a block across the room? What do you do when three-year-old Mary wants to do nothing but sit in your lap? What do you do when two-year-old Sally repeatedly gets off her cot during nap time?

Knowledge of how children develop will help, but no rules apply to *all* children at *all* stages of development. Each child is unique, and he or she must be understood in terms of his or her particular level of development and skills. Your reaction, therefore, should be based not only on your general knowledge of children of the same age, but also on your knowledge of the particular child, and the best guess you can make as to the causes of the particular behavior.

We believe that the material presented here will provide a solid basis for understanding children, and that you will want to continue gathering knowledge. It is likely that the more you learn, the more curious you will become, and the more interesting your chosen field will be to you. The challenges and responsibilities are many, but the satisfactions to be found in working with children are great.

Child Development for Day Care Workers

1

Principles and Theories of Development

After studying this chapter, you should be able to:

1. describe changes in body proportions between birth and six years of age
2. describe the *cephalocaudal* and *proximodistal trends* in motor development
3. describe the following elements of Piaget's theory: *sensorimotor* and *preoperational periods, assimilation,* and *accommodation*
4. considering Erikson's theory of personality development, describe behavior that shows evidence of *trust, autonomy,* and *initiative*
5. describe the steps in *behavior modification*

1

Several principles and theories of development are discussed briefly in this chapter to give a basis for understanding their application in the later chapters on infants, toddlers, and preschool children. At first, theories may not seem very useful in your daily work. You may wish that we had provided rules that could be used with every child in every situation, but this is impossible. No set of rules can apply to all children and all situations. Learning to use the theories discussed in this chapter in making daily decisions will help you in working with children under age six.

Growth of the Body

You may have heard the statement that children are not miniature adults. Comparing the body proportions of newborn infants with those of adults proves this fact. Newborns are top-heavy—their heads account for one-fourth of their total body length, as compared with one-eighth of the body length in adults. When you compare the lengths of newborns and adults, you see that legs make up one-fourth the total body length of the newborns and one-half the length of the adults. It fol-

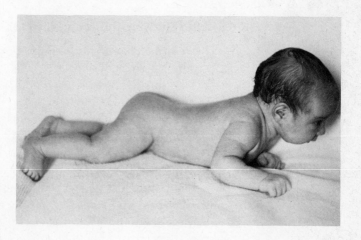

lows, then, that legs increase more rapidly in length than does the rest of the body from birth to adulthood. Children's rapid leg growth influences the way they control their bodies and develop motor skills.

TRENDS IN MOTOR DEVELOPMENT

Changing body proportions during the first six years mean that children's centers of gravity also change. Note the difference in the posture of toddlers walking with their legs far apart, in contrast with five-year-olds skipping with grace. Learning to cope with this changing body is an important process during these years.

Children of the same age vary in size, but body proportions are similar, and this shows a "built-in" plan of development. *Motor development*—the growth of skills for handling the body—provides further evidence for the unfolding ground plan. For example, all infants can control the upper part of the body before they can control the legs in walking. Infants never learn to walk before they can hold up their heads or sit alone. The sequence remains the same regardless of the specific age at which children learn these skills.

This sequence in developing control of the body is called the *cephalocaudal trend.* ("Cephalo" comes from the Greek word meaning "head" and "caudal," from the Latin word meaning "tail.")

Proximodistal trend refers to the development from the center to the edge of the body. "Proximal" means that part of the arm or leg that is closest to the point of attachment to the body. "Distal" describes the portion that is farthest from the body. Infants usually can reach toward and strike at a one-inch cube before they are six months old. But they cannot pick up the cube with their thumbs and forefingers until they are nearly a year old. Even at the end of the preschool period, children are awkward in using their fingers in dressing and in art activities. For example, most children cannot tie a bow or a knot until they are around five years old.

The age at which children are capable of specific motor skills depends both on the individuals' particular built-in plans of development and on the environment. For example, children who have not had chances to practice sitting and standing walk later than children who are given freedom of movement.[1] Adults do not need to teach children to walk; adults should help children learn to walk by providing freedom to explore, and praise for each new skill.

MATURATION AND PAST EXPERIENCE

What children are like at any given age depends on biological changes taking place according to their built-in plans (generally called *maturation*). What they are like also depends on their prior experiences. The children who were below average weight at birth (often called premature) may be expected to walk later than the children who were average or above average weight at birth. This is because their bodies need more time to develop to the point at which they are ready to walk. Severe illness may also slow the growth rate for a while, though after recovery children usually grow more rapidly.

UNEVENNESS OF DEVELOPMENT

We have noted that different parts of the body grow at different rates. This principle also holds true in development of skills. While children make important steps forward in one area, they may make little progress in another.

Unevenness can be seen in the development of large- and small-muscle control. Large muscles are involved in learning to walk, run, and climb. Control of small muscles is involved in the use of fingers. The ability to pick up an object with a pincer movement, using the thumb and first finger, appears toward the end of the first year, usually before infants learn to walk. For the next few years, they make rapid progress in running and stair-

climbing, but little progress, by comparison, in the use of their fingers.

INTERRELATEDNESS OF ALL ASPECTS OF DEVELOPMENT

Children's overall development is so complex that it is necessary to discuss one area at a time. This may lead you to think that each area can be considered separately, which is not true. The influence of one part of the body on another is evident, for example, when you remember how a headache influenced your performance on a difficult examination.

Infants who feel no pain will have more time to examine the environment and learn from it than infants who suffer from colic. Children's thinking ability affects their ability to perceive social situations. Their reactions to peers make a difference in their willingness to reach out to new learning experiences, especially in groups, as in a day care center. Being able to communicate thoughts and feelings influences relationships between children and adults. The children's ability to think and solve problems significantly influences all aspects of their behavior.

Development of Thought

Development of the ability to think logically, like physical growth, follows a pattern of development that begins in the first year of life. Since ability to think logically about a problem is less obvious than physical growth and motor skills, we are just beginning to understand how thinking develops in infants and children. The more we know about children's ability to understand everyday problems, like the difference between one apple and five apples, the more able we are to plan experiences that contribute to the development of logical thought.

Since children are not born with the ability to think

logically, they constantly try to make sense out of their experiences. Jean Piaget, a Swiss genetic epistemologist, has contributed many ideas about children's thinking. "Genetic epistemology deals with the formation and meaning of knowledge and with the means by which the human mind goes from a lower level of knowledge to one that is judged to be higher."[2] Piaget also assumes that biological maturation is important for development of children's thought processes.

His theory describes the changes in children's thinking from early in the first year of life to the time in early adolescence when most individuals are capable of logical thought. Development of thought is discussed in four stages, the first two of which describe development of thinking in children under ages six to seven. Piaget points out that the age range for these periods is approximate, varying for individual children. Experience influences the age at which children move from one stage to another.[3]

SENSORIMOTOR PERIOD

This period, which covers the first eighteen to twenty-four months of life, can be called the period of practical intelligence that precedes language. The relation of biological maturation to development of thinking is clearly evident during this period. Changes in infants' thinking take place through seeing, hearing, touching, smelling, and tasting. When infants can focus their eyes on an object and grasp it (around four and one-half months of age) they vastly increase their opportunities for learning because they can then grasp, taste, and manipulate the objects that come within their reach.

Two important milestones of the sensorimotor period are development of *object and person permanence* and the ability to form *hypotheses* (unproved guesses about the solution of a problem). Object permanence refers to the understanding that an object exists even though infants do not see it. You can determine whether infants have developed object permanence by noticing whether or not they look down for objects they have dropped. This concept seems so basic to adult thinking that it is difficult to comprehend how surroundings would appear if we all thought that people and objects only existed when we could see them. Person permanence (awareness that people exist when out of sight) is important in the development of infants' relationships with parents and caregivers.

The ability to form hypotheses, the second important achievement of the sensorimotor period, is the ability to think of solutions to a problem instead of arbitrarily trying one solution and then another until the problem is solved. We observe infants reaching and trying to move toward an object, then grasping the corner of the blanket under the object, pulling it toward them, and finally grasping what they had been trying to reach. This appears to be trial-and-error learning. Piaget describes a child trying to get a thimble out of a matchbox. First the child tries without success to get his fingers into the slightly open box, stopping to examine the situation as he opens and closes his hand. Then suddenly he slips his finger into the crack in the box so that it opens and he can get the thimble. With this second try, the child appears to have thought through the solution, or formed a hypothesis, before actually trying to remove the thimble.[4]

PREOPERATIONAL PERIOD

Forming hypotheses becomes easier during the *preoperational period*, which extends from around two to seven years of age, for children are now able to use language in thinking.

During the preoperational period, children become so skillful in communicating with adults that we might assume, incorrectly, that they think as adults do. But two deficiencies in children's thinking at this stage—lack of *reversibility* in thinking and *egocentricism*—demonstrate that this assumption is wrong.

An interesting way to test children's capacity for reversibility in thinking is through the *conservation problem*. You can carry out this experiment informally when you are playing with a child, using clay or play dough. Ask the child to make two balls of the same size. Then, as the child watches you, flatten the ball to make it look like a pancake. Ask the child whether the amount of clay in the ball and in the pancake is the same. Most preschool children will say "no" and indicate that the pancake is larger. When children say "yes" and can explain that nothing was added or taken away when the shape of the ball was changed, they show ability to conserve. This is evidence for reversibility in their thinking. They show that they can think of that pancake being rolled back into the same ball of clay. Until they are able to do this, telling them that ball and pancake have the same amount of clay will not influence their thinking. Of course, they can memorize the correct answer without changing their thinking.

Egocentricism is the inability to see a situation from another's point of view. You can demonstrate this deficiency in the preschool child's thinking by the following experiment. Face a child across a table set with placemats and with a fork and spoon at the child's place. Ask him or her to stay in place but to reach across the table and put the fork and spoon on your placemat. In situations like this, children will arrange the eating utensils as they would for themselves, because they think only of themselves.

Egocentricism often frustrates adults who work with children. How many times do adults have to interrupt a story group because three- or four-year-olds will sit down in the group directly in front of other children? They are not trying to upset the story group; they want to see the pictures and do not realize that they are keeping other children from seeing. They may further interrupt the story with a comment totally unrelated to the story, like "Look at my new shoes." In spite of adult talk about giving everyone an opportunity to see the pictures at story time, this type of behavior may occur frequently during this period, because all children consider only themselves most of the time.

Reversibility in thinking and less egocentricism in thinking show that children have moved into the next period, concrete operations. Formal thinking, the final state in development of thought, is reached around age twelve.

ASSIMILATION AND ACCOMMODATION

The concepts of *assimilation* and *accommodation* are useful in explaining how children move from one stage of thought to another in their day-to-day experiences. Assimilation is the process of incorporating new experiences into ideas or actions the children already have acquired. An eighteen-month-old child grabs and throws a plastic glass from her high chair after she has finished drinking her milk. At her grandfather's house, she has a breakable glass. She throws it, and it makes a loud noise and breaks into pieces. She frowns, looks puzzled, then cries.

This is assimilation: the child used the action, with the new glass, that she previously learned with another glass. Because the second glass did not produce the same results as the plastic one, the infant will have to change her ideas and her actions. This change is called accommodation. The next time this infant may at least hesitate before she throws a glass, because she knows that all glasses are not the same.

Each time children assimilate, then accommodate to, a new experience, they move one step toward the next stage in development of logical thought. Observing infants and young children over a period of time will give you many examples of this process at work.

Relationships with Others

Children's feelings about themselves and their relationships with other people are influenced by their capacity for logical thinking. For example, conflicts between children, and between children and adults, result from the children's inability to see other points of view. The fifteen-month-old snatches a doll from another child because he wants it. He often appears surprised when the other child protests and the adult frowns in disapproval. But the theory of egocentricism does not explain many childish behaviors that adults find baffling and often, irritating.

Erik Erikson's theory of personality development is useful in understanding children's regard for themselves and their behavior with others at different age levels. Like Piaget, in his theory of thought development, Erikson describes personality development using a series of stages extending from birth to death, each stage building on the preceding one. The three stages that cover the period from birth to six years are discussed here, with examples of relevant day care situations. The other stages are described briefly, to show how development during the years before six may affect development at a later age.

SENSE OF TRUST

Learning to trust oneself and others begins in infancy. This sense of trust, developed during the first year, depends on the quality of children's care.[5] Responding to infants' cries and planning for their physical comfort promote a sense of trust. To keep infants comfortable, you need to respect each one's unique physiological rhythms of eating, sleeping, and eliminating.

A certain amount of consistency in care is necessary because infants need to learn that adults are dependable. They also need adults who cuddle them, talk to them, and play with them. The infants whose care is shared by the staff in a day care center and their parents may have an advantage over those who remain at home, if needs in both situations are met by parents and center staff who communicate well with each other. Workers in the center can focus completely on the infants in their care because they are not distracted by the other tasks parents have at home. However, if the staff is extremely busy—if they are responsible for so many children that they cannot respond promptly to cries from one child— infants may have more difficulty developing trust. Basic trust also suffers when all infants are expected to eat and sleep at the same time, and when staff members do not have time to talk with parents.

According to Erikson, "This (referring to a sense of trust) forms the basis in the child for a sense of identity which will later combine a sense of being 'all right,' of being oneself, and of becoming what other people trust one will become."[6] Building on a sense of trust and moving toward a sense of identity, children move next to a sense of *autonomy* during the second and third years of life.

SENSE OF AUTONOMY

Autonomy means a sense of independence and, at the same time, ability to accept and use the help and guidance of others. During this period, children are developing many new skills—walking, climbing, dropping, pushing, pulling. They take great pride in these new skills. Their joy in their new-found independence is obvious. Notice the toddler when she is called by an adult: she runs a short distance away, then turns around with a grin on her face. She doesn't really want to avoid the adult; she is just enjoying her freedom to run away if she pleases.

One- to three-year-old children want to do many self-care activities like eating and dressing without help. They often make outrageous demands on themselves when a task is obviously impossible. This behavior tests the patience of adults.

Guidance to encourage autonomy should consist of helping children experience the thrill of independence while they learn to live within their limitations. The way this guidance is carried out is important. According to

Erikson, "Outer control at this stage, therefore, must be firmly reassuring."[7] For example, climbing on tables must be stopped, but children can be redirected to climbing equipment without being made to feel guilty.

Toilet training experience may be significant in children's development of autonomy, since control of elimination relates to children's feelings about their ability to control their bodies. Toilet training itself, however, is often more important to adults, than to children. Gradual toilet training when children seem ready, with emphasis on praise for success rather than shame for failure, is important for a developing sense of autonomy.

The children in the day care center may have fewer limitations to face on their attempts at independence because toilets, tables, and chairs are the right size for them and materials within reach are not potentially dangerous. They may have more opportunity to be guided into acceptable activities instead of doing the unacceptable at home and being criticized by busy parents.

However, children in the center may have difficulty in establishing feelings of independence and capability if kinds of behavior permitted at the center are different from those permitted at home. Parents and center staff can work together toward being consistent in demands. Limits that differ because of the situation can be explained. For example, you can point out to children that it is all right to play in water in the sink at school, but their parents do not like them to play in the sink at home.

SENSE OF INITIATIVE

Having established a sense of trust and a sense of autonomy, children are ready to establish a sense of *initiative* during the years between three and six. "Initiative adds to autonomy the quality of undertaking, planning and 'attacking' a task for the sake of being active and on the move, where before self-will, more often than not, inspired acts of defiance, or at any rate protested independence."[8]

For children, this is a period of enterprise and imagination. An activity characteristic of a developing sense of initiative is dreaming of big projects without much concern for the skills or materials needed to carry them out. Adults may be worried by children's rapid shift from one project to another, and their lack of ability to assess their skills. Children will grow in their ability to evaluate their work realistically during the next stage, when they develop a sense of industry. While developing a sense of initiative, children need space, materials, and encouragement to try out their ideas. A day care center can often provide these more easily than can the home.

PERSONALITY DEVELOPMENT AFTER AGE SIX

The remaining steps in Erikson's theory of personality development are described briefly here, to show how development during the first six years influences development later in life. At each stage, development is influenced not just by experience at that particular time, but also by development that occurred earlier in life.

Sense of industry. A sense of industry, developing during the school years (six to twelve), builds on children's sense of initiative. Children grow in their ability to plan projects that more nearly fit their skills and materials, and they do more evaluating of their work. Their growing ability to reason and to learn to follow rules contributes to their success in school. Children are more important to each other and they are more likely to be involved in projects together. Learning to work out a division of labor is an accomplishment of this stage.

Sense of identity. Having established a sense of confidence in their ability to work, children come to the end of childhood and enter adolescence (twelve to eighteen).

The achievement of this stage is the development of a sense of identity. Identity has been defined as "a sense of who he is, where he has been, and where he is going."[9] While all preceding stages are important, a sense of trust and a sense of autonomy are crucial in establishing a sense of identity. Identity is important for the next step, a sense of intimacy.

Sense of intimacy. This stage extends from late adolescence to early middle age. During this stage, individuals gain the ability to share with and care about other individuals without losing the sense of identity. Usually this involves selection of marriage partners, but a sense of intimacy involves close relationships with persons of either sex.

Sense of generativity. This stage, which extends from middle to old age, can be described as the ability to be concerned about other people beyond one's immediate family. It includes concern for future generations. Rearing children is an important experience of this period. Like the final stage, a sense of integrity, generativity builds on all the stages that preceded it.

Sense of integrity. A sense of integrity may be defined as the individual's ability to look back on life with satisfaction. Individuals who have developed the sense of integrity are not afraid of death. While a sense of trust is basic to all the preceding steps in personality development, the sense of trust established in infancy seems particularly significant in this final step.

To simplify the theory, only the positive parts of each stage have been included here. Each stage has a negative component—e.g., mistrust versus trust. While each stage builds on what happened earlier in life, Erikson does not propose that a component, such as trust established in the first year, cannot be modified by later experiences. The theory suggests that if a strong sense of trust is not established during the first year, it is more difficult to develop into a trusting person later in life.

16

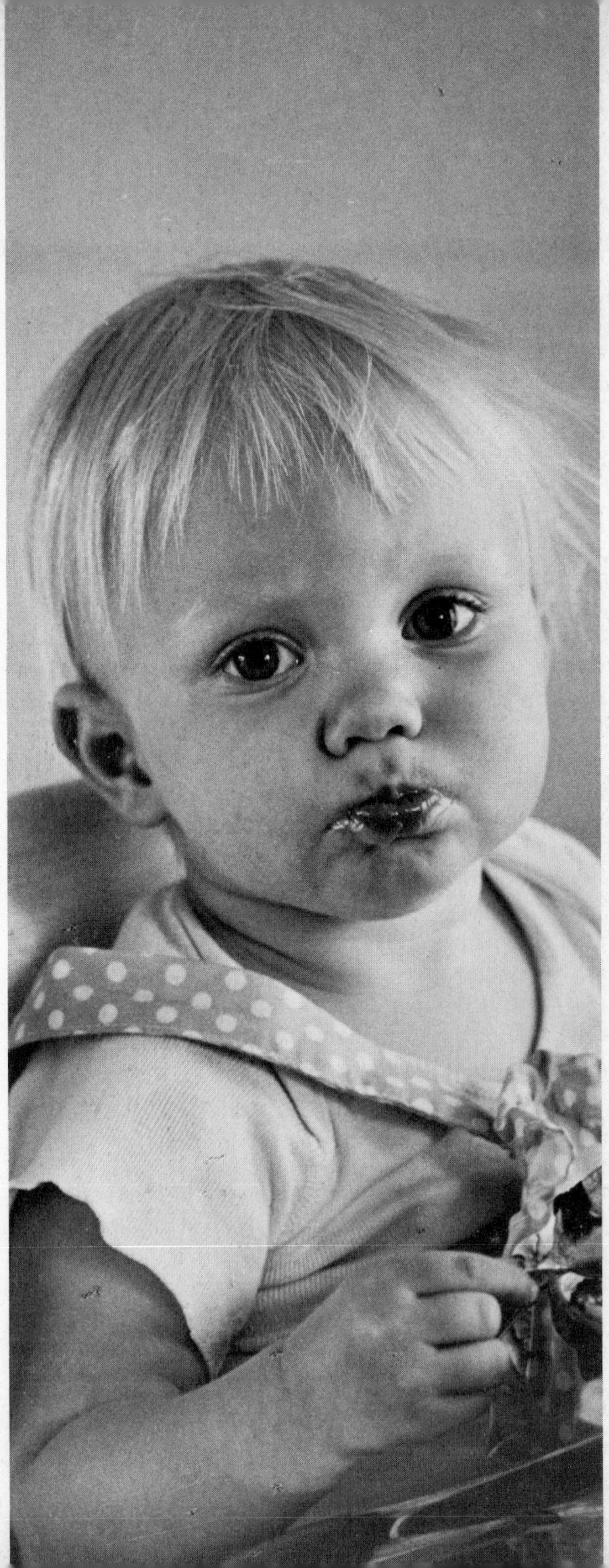

Behaviorism

Behaviorism is an important theory in psychology. It emphasizes the importance of learning in understanding human behavior. It also stresses the importance of observing behavior in order to understand individuals. *Behavior modification*, a technology that has grown out of behaviorism, is particularly important to those who work with young children.

Behavior modification is based on the assumption that animals and human beings repeat behavior that brings satisfaction. Behavior modification has always been used to some extent by adults who live with young children. Over the years, parents have learned from their parents that children will repeat behaviors that have been praised. However, behavior modification involves a systematic approach to changing behavior.

The first step in behavior modification is systemati-

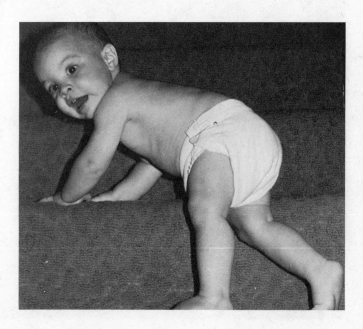

cally to record the frequency over a period of time of the behavior that interests the adult. For example, take a four-year-old who sits and watches in the day care center but rarely uses blocks or other play materials indoors. Here adults would need to record over a specified period of time the number of minutes the child sits and watches. The adults would then decide on the reinforcement, usually the attention of a preferred adult. The adult who had a close relationship with the child would approach and give the child special attention each time she made any attempt to enter an activity. At first, the adult would reward *any* attempt. Later, as the child's behavior changed, the adult would give attention only when the child was definitely involved in an activity. At the same time, all adults would ignore the child when she was merely watching.

Behavior modification gives adults considerable power to change children's behavior. With power goes responsibility; when using behavior modification, you must think carefully about the effect the behavior change will have on the children and their families. A behavior may be annoying to adults but of real importance to the children. It is possible to teach toddlers not to "get into everything," but changing this behavior extensively robs the children of an important way to learn.

In this chapter we have discussed patterns of physical growth and applied principles of development to learning control of the body. We also have described one theory of how children learn to think and solve problems and one theory of personality development. And we have briefly described a method for changing behavior. There are other theories about children's development, and undoubtedly new theories will be formed in the future.

Knowledge of principles of development increases our awareness of developing skills of children at different age levels. Understanding theories helps us accept puzzling and sometimes irritating behavior and provides a basis for determining when we should try to change it.

Glossary

Accommodation   In Piaget's theory, a concept describing changes in an individual's existing ideas or actions as a result of the process of assimilation.

Assimilation   In Piaget's theory, a concept describing an individual's incorporating a new experience into ideas or actions already acquired.

Autonomy   In Erikson's theory of personality development, the second stage, covering the second and third years of life, when children develop a sense of independence along with the ability to use the help and guidance of others.

Behaviorism   Psychological theory that emphasizes learning.

Behavior modification   Technology outlining strategy for changing behavior.

Cephalocaudal trend   Sequence in which infants gain control of their bodies, proceeding from head to lower part of the body.

Conservation problem   Test of the child's ability to recognize that a quantity remains the same when it changes shape or position.

Egocentricism   A thinking deficiency in all young children, who are concerned with self, looking at all things in relation to themselves.

Hypotheses   Unproved guesses about the solution of a problem.

Initiative   In Erikson's theory, the third stage of development, covering third through the fifth years of life. Children develop the ability to formulate plans and carry them out without much concern for their skills.

Learning   Changes in behavior due to experience.

Maturation   Developmental changes appearing with increase in age and relatively independent of environmental factors.

Motor development   Changing abilities in control of the body, such as walking, climbing, grasping, and handling objects.

Object or person permanence   Awareness that people and
   objects exist even when the infant cannot see them.

Physical environment   Space and materials available to
   children in their surroundings.

Preoperational period   In Piaget's theory, the stage covering the period from two to six years of age. It
   differs from the preceding stage in that children are
   able to use language in thinking.

Proximodistal trend   A sequence in development in which
   infants gain control of their bodies, proceeding
   from center to periphery of the body.

Reversibility   The ability to think about the logical consequences of retracing a line of reasoning back to its
   beginning. Understanding that flattening a ball of
   clay does not alter the amount of clay is an example
   of reversibility.

Sensorimotor period   In Piaget's theory, the first stage,
   covering the first two years of life. Learning at this
   stage takes place through the senses and manipulation of materials.

Trust   In Erikson's theory of personality development,
   the first stage, covering the first year of life. Infants
   develop confidence in themselves and others.

Study Questions

1. Observe an infant in a nursery of newborns in a
   hospital or a young infant in a home, noting size of
   head as compared to length of legs. Compare with a
   preschool child.
2. Carry out a conservation experiment with a three- to
   five-year-old child and report the results. This can be
   done with clay, as described in the text, or with two
   glasses of water and a glass bowl. Have the child pour
   the same amount of water in two glasses, then pour
   the water from one glass into a glass bowl, and pro-

ceed with questioning as in conservation experiment with clay.

3. Observe a one- to two-year-old child for an hour. List behaviors you saw which give evidence that the child is developing a sense of autonomy.

4. Observe preschool children in a day care center for at least one hour. Describe a child you consider to have developed a strong sense of initiative and one who has not.

5. In a day care center, assist a staff member who wants to modify a behavior of a particular child utilizing modification. Be responsible for recording the frequency of the behavior before and after the plan for changing behavior has been put into effect.

Notes

1. W. Dennis, "Infant Development under Conditions of Restricted Practice and Minimum of Social Stimulation," *Genetic Psychology Monographs, 23* (1941), p. 182.

2. J. Piaget, "Genetic Epistemology," in *Annual Editions Readings in Human Development* '73–'74, Dushkin Publishing Group, Guilford, Connecticut, 1973, p. 41.

3. J. Piaget and B. Inhelder, *The Psychology of the Child*, Basic Books, New York, 1969, p. 153.

4. *Ibid.*, p. 12.

5. E. Erikson, *Childhood and Society*, 2nd ed. Norton, New York, 1963, p. 249.

6. *Ibid*, p. 249.

7. *Ibid.*, p. 252.

8. *Ibid.*, p. 255.

9. D. Elkind, "Erik Erikson's Eight Stages of Man," *Annual Editions Readings in Human Development* '73–'74, Dushkin Publishing Group, Guilford, Connecticut, 1973, p. 27.

Supplementary Readings

Elkind, D. "Giant in the Nursery—Jean Piaget." In *Annual Editions Readings in Human Development* '73–'74. Dushkin Publishing Group, Guilford, Connecticut, 1973.

Wadsworth, B. J. *Piaget's Theory of Cognitive Development.* David McKay, New York, 1971.

2

The
First
Year
of
Life

After reading this chapter, you should be able to:

1. discuss the rapid rate of change in appearance and behavior during the first year
2. predict probable characteristic behavior of the infant at zero to one month, two to three months, four to six months, seven to nine months, and ten to twelve months
3. select materials and activities most likely to gain the attention of the infant at each level of development
4. discuss the significance of *attachment*, *stranger anxiety*, and *separation anxiety* for the infant in day care
5. trace language development from the birth cry to the first spoken words
6. explain to a parent how and why play is a means of learning for the infant
7. describe how infant behavior is shaped through *modeling*, *redirection*, and *reinforcement*
8. outline ways a professional worker can influence the development of the infant

In this book *infancy* is defined as the period from birth to the first birthday. The upper limit is set at one year, when most infants have learned some form of locomotion—crawling, walking, or a combination of the two. At that age, infants are capable of moving about on their own, and a new dimension enters into the caregiving procedure. However, any division of development by age level is artificial because of the wide range in the rate of individual development.

Because of this wide variation, descriptions of characteristic behavior at different age levels must be applied cautiously. The characteristic behavior outlined in Table 1 and discussed in the following section is based on observation of a limited number of infants. *These landmarks of development are not to be used as criteria to evaluate a particular infant's development.* They are intended to provide a general basis of comparison for your observations as you work with infants of different ages. They will also aid you in selecting materials and activities best suited to help infants develop their skills at different levels of development.

As you follow infants from birth to the first birthday or observe groups of infants at different age levels, you will be impressed by the rapid changes in appearance and skills. At no other period in life do changes occur as rapidly as during the first year. The birth weight of average infants almost triples and length increases by about nine inches. Infants develop from newborns, whose behavior consists entirely of reflexes such as sucking, swallowing, crying, and grasping, into individuals capable of expressing needs and feelings and of solving simple problems.

Landmarks of Development

BIRTH TO ONE MONTH

According to Table 1, the average weight at birth is seven to eight pounds. Birth weight is of some sig-

TABLE 1 *Landmarks of Infant Development*

PHYSICAL, MOTOR, AND LANGUAGE DEVELOPMENT	SOCIAL DEVELOPMENT
0–1 month	
Birth size: 7–8 pounds, 20 inches	Helpless
Feedings: 5–7 per day	Asocial
Sensory capacities: makes basic distinctions in vision, hearing, smelling, tasting, touch temperature, and perception of pain	Generalized tension
Reflexes: sucks, swallows, cries, hiccoughs, grasps	
2–3 months	
Sensory capacities: color perception, visual exploration, oral exploration	Visually fixates on a face
Sounds: cries, coos, grunts	Smiles at a face
Motor ability: controls eye muscles, lifts head when on stomach	May be soothed by rocking
4–6 months	
Sensory capacities: localizes sounds	Expects feeding, dressing, bathing
Sounds: babbling, makes most vowels and about half of the consonants	Recognizes mother .
Feedings: 3–5 per day	Distinguishes between familiar persons and strangers
Motor ability: controls head and arm movements, grasps, rolls over	No longer smiles indiscriminately
	Enjoys being cuddled
7–9 months	
Motor ability: controls trunk and hands, sits without support, crawls (abdomen touching floor)	Develops specific emotional attachment to one or more caregivers
	Protests separation from mother or chief caregiver
	Enjoys "peek-a-boo"
10–12 months	
Motor ability: controls legs and feet, stands, creeps, uses pincer grasp of thumb and forefinger	Expresses anger and affection
	Expresses fear of strangers
Language: says one or two words, imitates sounds, responds to simple commands	Develops curiosity, explores
	Responds to own name
Feedings: 3 meals, 2 snacks	Understands "no-no"
Size at one year: 20 pounds, 29 inches	Waves "bye-bye"
	Plays "pat-a-cake"

SOURCE: Adapted from Boyd R. McCandless and Ellis D. Evans, *Children and Youth: Psychosocial Development,* Dryden Press, Hinsdale, Illinois, 1973, p. 12, and Charles P. Smith, *Child Development,* William C. Brown, New York, 1966, pp. 8–9. Reprinted by permission of Dryden Press and Charles P. Smith.

nificance to the person who works with infants and pre-school children because it has been shown to be connected with rate of development. For example, studies have shown that until as late as four years of age, infants of low birth weight (less than five pounds) generally remain smaller and obtain lower scores on tests of cognitive and motor development than infants of average birth weight.[1]

Newborns are remarkably capable organisms. All senses, with the possible exception of taste, are well developed at birth, and taste develops soon after birth.[2] Although newborns are capable of focusing their eyes only momentarily, they do react to bright light in contrast to darkness. The sense of touch can be observed in the *rooting reflex* (turning the head and sucking when the cheek is stroked).

One noticeable physical characteristic of newborns is the inability to control the head. For the first two to three months of life, the head must be supported when infants are picked up or held.

During the first month infants who make a comfortable adjustment to life outside the uterus spend a great deal of time sleeping. This is a shallow sleep, broken up by many brief waking periods. Even when awake, children of this age do not react to caregiving people, but rather to the fulfillment or neglect of their needs.

TWO TO THREE MONTHS

By the end of the second month, average infants are showing more interest in the environment and smiling at many of the human faces they see. They demonstrate increasing control of the head by an ability to raise the chest and hold up the head when lying on the stomach.

Infants of two to three months often coo, cry and grunt in sequence. Though language development could be said to begin with the birth cry, the *cooing* characteristic of this age seems more like the beginning of language to adults.

During this period the infants demonstrate the beginnings of sociability. They seem to enjoy being held briefly and hearing an adult gently talk and sing to them. For some infants, the environment changes from home to the day care center toward the end of this period. As compared with infants who are older when they're placed in the center, infants of this age seem to adjust to the center with greater acceptance of new caregivers and less sense of loss of mothers or previous caregivers.

FOUR TO SIX MONTHS

Between four and six months of age infants usually begin to sit, first with support and later without it. This achievement enables them to see more of their environment and to look at their surroundings from a different perspective. Infants now begin *babbling*, which, in contrast to cooing, involves making specific sounds that are still not recognizable words. As indicated in Table 1, four- to six-month-old infants can make most vowel and half the consonant sounds.

Infants use their eyes, hands, and mouths to explore the environment. They can pick up an object within reach with a raking motion, though the thumb and first finger are not yet useful. Much of what they grasp, including toys, clothes, and toes, goes into their mouths.

Four- to six-month-old infants show signs of recognizing their mothers and other familiar adults and begin to show different responses to strangers. Attachment to mother or to a significant adult, as well as distress on separation from these adults and fear of strangers, becomes more obvious during the next age period.

SEVEN TO NINE MONTHS

For many infants this can be the period of strongest protest on separation from mother if they have been cared for primarily by her up to this point. Admission to the day care center at this time may not be desirable if infants react this way.

Infants of seven to nine months have a great variety of skills. They begin to experiment with some form of locomotion—creeping, crawling, walking with support, and for a few, walking alone. At this age, infants may be able to stand up in the crib or *play yard*, but may begin to cry because they do not know how to get down. By the end of this period, many infants are more efficient in picking up objects because they can make the pincer movement with thumb and first finger. They can coordinate well enough to hold objects like small blocks in each hand and bang them together. If they have the opportunity, these infants will look at themselves in the mirror, smiling at and patting their images.

Seven- to nine-month-old infants show signs of being aware that people and objects exist even when they are out of sight. As Chapter 1 explained, Piaget has called this ability object permanence. At this point, infants are ready for games like "peek-a-boo" and "bye-bye."

TEN TO TWELVE MONTHS

Interaction with infants becomes even more interesting during this period, because they begin to vocalize with words like "da-da" and "ma-ma." Their understanding of many words is evident in their ability to follow simple directions, such as "Show me your shoes."

Object permanence has developed by now. One game common among children of this age involves dropping an object, listening to the sound when the object hits the floor, and waiting expectantly for an adult to pick it up. This game helps them understand space and serves as a basis for social interaction with adults.

Locomotion and small-muscle coordination also improve. Many infants can sit up, stand, and perhaps even sit down again without falling. Some can walk, either alone or holding onto a hand, by the end of this period.

Ten- to twelve-month-old infants are generally able to pick up small toys and pieces of food with thumb and index finger. This allows them to feed themselves finger food. Some babies can get food into their mouths with a spoon, though much of the food ends up on the face, table, and walls. These children can drink from cups, though not without some spilling, and they may throw or roll a ball.

Infants now are well on their way to being exploring toddlers. They examine things more closely with their eyes and fingers and do less mouthing of interesting objects. Their greater mobility makes it possible for them to explore an increasing number of objects and people.

Perceiving and Learning

Obviously, infants explore and learn from the environment at the end of the infancy period, but they learn through their senses from birth. What attracts and holds infants' attention is important to those who arrange their environment. We assume that experiences that bring about assimilation and accommodation (as defined in Piaget's theory in Chapter 1) contribute to infants' development of thought.

LEARNING THROUGH SEEING

During the first months of life, infants are learning to focus on objects at a distance. Up until about two months, their *visual accommodation* appears fixed and appropriate for objects about eight inches from the eyes.[3]

Researchers have devised clever methods to determine what kinds of objects and designs hold the attention of infants even before they have achieved distance vision. These findings provide some guidance in selecting objects infants are more likely to examine when they can see them.

Contrast seems to be important. Infants focus longer

on patterns that show black and white contrast than on a patch of gray.[4] From this, one might suppose that bright colors would be more likely to get infants' attention than the traditional pastel pink and blue. Findings with regard to specific colors are far from clear, but there is no conclusive evidence for a color preference among infants.[5]

Movement is important in gaining attention: even five-day-old babies momentarily stop sucking on nipples when a light moves into their visual field.[6] This explains why *mobiles* hold infants' attention for long periods of time. Both movement and contour are involved in infants' attraction to the human face. After the first few weeks of life, human figures, particularly faces, become increasingly able to attract attention.[7]

LEARNING THROUGH HEARING

Infants are most attentive to sounds that are moderately different from the familiar ones.[8] However, less is known about auditory perception than about vision in infants. Rhythmic sounds must gain attention, since they reduce crying,[9] as most parents have discovered. Sounds that last from five to fifteen seconds seem to have the greatest effect on newborns, and we might guess that this applies to older infants. Therefore, in the day care center, infants may be expected to pay closer attention to the sounds of music boxes, wind chimes, and crib sound-toys than to the constant, background sound of the record player.

OTHER SENSES

The other senses provide ways for learning, but research is lacking on touch, taste, smell, and the *kinesthetic sense*. Most infants react to hard or soft surfaces, toys with a variety of textures, objects that smell, and to being picked up, held, and cuddled. At least two studies with institutionalized infants showed that tactile stimulation increased the amount of time one group of infants spent exploring their environment with their eyes. When they were compared to a control group, they displayed superior performance in terms of infant development.[10]

Too many sights and sounds may not provide useful stimulation for infants. We feel that in some group care situations with ten or more infants in one room there may be so much noise and movement that individual children may have trouble focusing on the smile and words directed to them.

There may be a relationship between noise and fatigue, since some infants are highly sensitive to their surroundings. To protect such babies in the day care setting, you need certain precautions. Limit the number of infants in a room; use sound-absorbent ceilings and carpet where possible; and remove mobiles from sight when infants are getting irritable for no apparent reason. Also, you can take such infants outdoors, where there is less noise and less close-up visual stimulation.

LEARNING THROUGH PLAY

Infants also learn through the materials they manipulate and the verbal *games* they play with adults and other children. General considerations are given here for selecting toys for particular infants. (Lists of materials for infant day care centers have been developed in other publications.[11])

We have just discussed sights and sounds that are likely to attract attention. Toys that provide both sights and sounds, like a bright rattle or a ball with a bell inside, have some advantage over toys that appeal to only one sense. There even are a few books appropriate for older infants that focus on learning through sensory experience. For example, *Pat the Bunny* includes a soft bunny picture to pat, a mirror, a ring to try on, and a paper boy who plays "peek-a-boo."[12]

Toys must also be evaluated for their safety. Whether or not a toy is safe to be put into the mouth is important during the second six months of life, when most of what infants get into their hands goes into their mouths. Toys for this age group must be washable and if painted, painted with lead-free, nontoxic paints. Toys must not have any part or piece, like the button eyes on stuffed animals, that can be pulled off, put in the mouth, and swallowed.

The developmental level of infants is most important in toy selection and in the activities you provide. Though we have given you some guidelines, you must determine this for each infant in your care. Toys and activities should give infants opportunity to practice the skills they are beginning to develop. When they begin to reach for and grasp objects, they are ready for small balls and blocks to pick up. When they have gained the concept of person permanence, they are ready to play "peek-a-boo."

Person permanence and object permanence are concepts from Piaget's theory of cognitive development discussed in Chapter 1. The understanding that people and objects exist even when they are out of sight is a milestone in development during the sensorimotor period. "Hiding" games give infants the opportunity to use the concept of object permanence and to practice forming hypotheses. However, these traits are generally not well developed until toward the end of the first year, and therefore games involving hiding objects must begin with easy ones. Start by covering an object while the child watches, and then, when the child seems ready, progress to hiding the object in another part of the room when the child is not looking.

Language Development

With the birth cry, the infant starts active breathing and makes his first attempt to communicate. During the first year, the style of communication changes from month to month.

We have mentioned that the cooing and grunting of

the second and third months give way to more specific babbling during the four- to six-month age period.

The first sounds are vowel-like such as [i] and [u], produced in the front of the mouth. Infants younger than three months also make consonant sounds like [k] and [g] that are produced in the back of the mouth. As more sounds are added, babies produce consonant sounds closer to the front of the mouth and vowel sounds from the back of the mouth.[13]

In contrast to the trend in the appearance of first sounds, the first meaningful speech sounds such as "da-da" are made up of front consonants and back vowels. Even more interesting is the fact that these combinations of sounds (front consonants and back vowels) are the starting point for meaningful speech in every language, whether it is English, Swedish, or Japanese.[14]

Environment does influence the use and continued practice of infants' spontaneous vocalizations. According to one theory, infants are reinforced by hearing their own vocalizations.[15] There is support for this theory in the observation that the range of sounds made by deaf children decreases gradually after the age of six months, even though their vocalizations were similar to those of hearing children prior to that time.[16] Contact with adults also affects vocalization in infants. Rheingold and others showed that an adult could increase vocalizations of four-to six-month-old infants with a smile, a sound, and a light touch on the abdomen.[17]

Infants can generally understand more words than they use in speech, as shown by their responses to commands (although they may depend to some extent on nonverbal cues.) Toward the end of the infancy period and through the toddler period, caregivers can influence this *passive vocabulary* by naming objects as children touch them, or describing activities: "We climb up the stairs." Even though human beings have a built-in capacity to develop speech, adults can help infants develop the sounds they make and the sounds they hear into an effective system of communication.

Attachment

Significant adults play an important role in the development of language, but they are absolutely central in the development of *attachment*, *stranger anxiety*, and *separation anxiety*. The concept of attachment, borrowed from *ethology* (the study of animal behavior), has been defined as children's tendency to approach or remain close to certain people, usually the mother or a limited number of caregivers.

Infants go through three stages in establishing attachment.[18] During the first two months of life, they show as much interest in inanimate objects as in human beings. Between the ages of two to six or seven months of age, they are more responsive to people than to the rest of their environment but are equally responsive to all people. At the third stage, infants show a preference for a few select people. They are receptive to being cared for by these particular people and least afraid when with them. For most children, this attachment behavior declines during the second and third years of life but may be expected to continue into the preschool years.[19] (This child-to-parent attachment is only one of a series of attachment relationships throughout the life span. Others are the husband-to-wife and parent-to-child attachments.)

Formation of attachment is one example of the influence of thought processes on social relationships. To form an attachment, infants first must develop the ability to see and remember the differences between their parents or preferred adults and other adults. They must also achieve the concept of person permanence to understand that the parent or preferred adult exists even when out of sight.

Attachment shows a child's increased maturity, and it gives rise to certain fears—fear of strangers, or stranger anxiety, and distress on separation from the attached figure, or separation anxiety. On the average, these fears are most obvious between nine and twelve months of age.[20]

Implications for Day Care

Research findings on infant attachment, stranger anxiety, and separation anxiety are particularly important in day care. It is not wise to apply blindly findings that are far from conclusive to practical day-to-day care of infants, but responsible professional people should combine the information with day-to-day observation of infants in their care, after which they can make judicious decisions about care.

DAY CARE AND ATTACHMENT

Knowing about attachment, stranger anxiety, and separation anxiety can ease the stress on both parents and children in planning enrollment in a day care center. Many states now permit group care of infants in situations where there are enough adults to provide individualized care and stimulation. This policy change in licensing centers was based on research surveys that indicated that lack of responsiveness and retardation in motor and language development in infants reared in orphanages was due to lack of stimulation rather than to absence of a mother-infant tie.[21]

There is evidence that infants form strong attachments to their mothers even when they are not constantly with them. A recent study that compared home-reared American children and Israeli children in a kibbutz showed that in the third year of life the Israeli children, who had been separated frequently from their parents from early infancy, were comparable to the American children on measures of attachment and separation anxiety.[22] A study of infants in day care found no difference in attachment behaviors between infants who had been in group infant care and those who had been reared at home.[23]

When considering the placement of any child in a day care center, remember that age makes a difference in attachment behavior. On the average, infants who are separated from their parents may be more distressed during the last three months of the first year and the first three months of the second year. If there is a choice for age of enrollment, the period between three and six months, when infants seem to accept everybody, may be the better time. If admitted at this early age, children would be attached to both the chief caregiver at home and the chief caregiver in the center.

Infants appear to have the capacity to attach to a limited number of people. This means that it is important to have one person at the center responsible for a particular infant. This chief caregiver can provide more responsive care than a number of caregivers: the more you observe and work with a particular infant the better able you are to interpret the infant's individual communications.

The method used to introduce infants into the day care center is as important as their ages. Regardless of age, the mothers or fathers should stay with the infants in the center for at least a day. If children must enter the center when separation anxiety is high, the parents should expect to remain longer. Their presence can help the babies adjust to the center, ease their own fears, and provide useful information for the center staff, who can learn the infant's likes, dislikes, and particular communication signals. Parents can learn about experiences the infants will be having in the center, and some will gain useful information on infant care. Their continued presence provides time to build a relationship between parents and staff that will enable them to share effectively the care of the infants.

DAY CARE AND DEVELOPMENT OF A SENSE OF TRUST

Once in the center, care that respects infants' physiological rhythms contributes to their sense of trust in themselves and in the people around them. Providing individualized care is a challenge to the day care worker because infants of the same age vary widely in *physiological reactivity*, which generally is called *temperament*.

Temperament includes activity level, irritability, and passivity. Parents frequently talk about "good" babies—passive infants who put themselves on a schedule early in life, eating and sleeping with little fuss. Irritable infants, by contrast, seem to have trouble sleeping and eating at similar times from day to day. They need more time and attention to help them achieve the physiological comfort that seems to be essential to establishing a sense of trust.

Even for placid infants, planning for individualized care with regard to eating and sleeping requires some thought. Some babies are sleepers, content to nap off and on all day, only awakening to be fed, diapered, and cuddled back to sleep. Other babies seem ready to join the world on a twenty-four-hour-a-day basis and strongly resist napping and bedtime hours. (Younger infants generally sleep more than older infants.) Infants may have more difficulty in falling asleep during their adjustment period in the center.

A separate room for sleep helps in individualizing the sleeping routine, though infants can sleep in a noisy environment. A rocking chair is also useful when you must calm a tired, irritable, or frightened infant.

Parent-staff discussion of what the infants eat at the center is desirable, and frequently the infants' pediatricians are involved in recommending foods offered. You can expect some variation among pediatricians' recommendations, particularly in connection with timing and sequence of adding solid foods. Eating will be encouraged if similar foods are encountered in both environments. Also, knowing infants' hunger cries will help you know when they need to be fed. Prompt attention when children are hungry will contribute to their sense of trust, too. Especially helpful is arranging a *self-demand schedule* for feeding according to infants' observed needs.

Planning with parents is also necessary when changing the method of feeding, and here again pediatricians' advice may be involved. Beginning to drink from a cup is an example. An early start on drinking from a cup seems to ease giving up the bottle for many children. Most infants have the coordination for this skill around five months of age. Gradual transitions like this contribute positively to the development of a sense of trust.

Transition from being fed to self-feeding is often gradual because infants frequently attempt to feed themselves before adults want to let them take over the job. If you have watched eight- to twelve-month-old infants feed themselves, you understand why. Letting infants feed themselves demonstrates your confidence in them and contributes to their sense of trust. A feeding spoon (with ball bearing between bowl and handle to keep the spoon in a correct position) is helpful, along with a large bib, and plenty of newspapers on the floor.

Most infants seem to enjoy food and eat an amazing quantity. However, as infants become more interested in what is going on around them, they may have days when they are more interested in watching and entertaining adults than in eating. They may also vary from week to week in their likes and dislikes. A good general rule is, don't force an infant to eat. Eating can develop into a battle between infant and adult. Healthy children, offered a variety of foods and no chance to obtain sweets, should select what their bodies need.

Thumbsucking is related to eating and sleeping. Sucking seems to comfort a tired, hungry infant, and for some, it seems to shut out the surroundings and help them relax and to go sleep. Infants who are adjusting to the center may tend to suck their thumbs more, if it is an important source of comfort for them. Various explanations have been given for why some babies suck their thumbs and others don't, but no one explanation is generally accepted at the present time.

Substituting a pacifier for a thumb has the advantage that pacifiers generally are given up more readily than thumbs.[24] However, in group care, pacifiers are easily transferred from one infant to another, which is a distinct disadvantage. Parents may need help in understanding infants' need to suck their thumbs or pacifiers. It may be desirable to take time to explain the reasons for this behavior.

Elimination is another physiological function that needs to be mentioned in connection with trust. Permitting infants to eliminate according to their own time schedules also contributes to their feeling of trust in themselves. Sometimes it is possible to get a baby on the pot in time to catch a bowel movement, but in this situation the adult is trained, not the infant. Generally, the second half of the second year is the best time for toilet training. This will be discussed further in Chapter 3.

PLANNING FOR INFANT LEARNING

While you are meeting children's physiological needs, you can also help them learn about their relationships with people and things. Talking, singing, cuddling, patting, and rocking all provide important sensory experiences. These activities may ease the resistance of infants who seem to fight clothes- and diaper-changing during the second half of the first year. Taking time to talk to infants, giving them different toys to hold, or placing a *mobile* above the changing table makes the situation a learning experience instead of a battle.

One observational study of four-month-old girls with their mothers showed that "middle-class" mothers talked more to their infants when not doing anything else, while "lower-class" mothers talked most frequently during routine care.[25] One possible conclusion for vocabulary differences in similar groups of children at age two is that the infants who were talked to during routine care paid as much attention to the tactile stimulation as to the mothers' speech. Therefore, it may be important to talk to infants at times other than during routine care.

In time spent with infants outside routine care, you can introduce new games when infants are ready, look at pictures if they show interest, or explore different toys.

You may watch while they explore on their own. Being outside the crib and play yard, both indoors and out, gives infants added learning opportunities. The amount of time babies can safely spend together depends on the individual, the particular group of infants, and the number of adults available to protect them from harm.

GUIDANCE

Infants' behavior must be limited when they are in danger of being hurt or of hurting each other. The safer the environment, the less stress on both infants and adults. Toward the end of the first year, infants are learning the meaning of the word "no," but they are usually not able to stop behavior on this signal. When they are older, they will begin to learn by rules. During infancy, the adult must be responsible for stopping a behavior like pulling hair and redirecting the infants' attention to something else like favorite toys.

The Infant Caregiver

Working with infants requires physical stamina, a special sensitivity and respect for helpless human beings, and creativity in guessing what will comfort a crying infant. Physical stamina is important because so much lifting is required, and infants are more upset than older children when a caregiver is absent due to illness. With the physical stamina and constant watchfulness should go alertness. Once mobile, infants can get into danger spots with unbelievable speed. Severe falls or burns do not just hurt the children, they can also damage their sense of trust and their willingness to explore.

The importance of being willing to respond to infants' cries cannot be underestimated. One recent study showed that mothers who responded to their infants' cries in early infancy had infants who cried less at the

end of the first year than mothers who were less responsive.[26]

SELF-UNDERSTANDING

Recognizing your own feelings and having some understanding of why you react in a certain way can help you
in deciding whether you should work with infants or
with older children and will help in analyzing your relationships with individual children.

Many of us are unaware of our feelings toward certain
childish behavior until we come face to face with it in the
center. We all find certain kinds of behavior irritating
and other kinds of behavior appealing. Children who

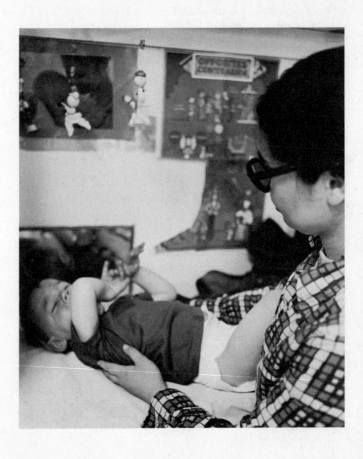

exhibit behavior that irritates you probably will seem less attractive.

People who say they love all children are only fooling themselves. No one of us can change feelings, but we can check on ourselves to see that we divide attention among all the infants in our care.

To work with infants, you need to know how much positive reinforcement—encouragement and moral support—you need from other people. Young babies make few contributions to the infant-adult relationship. The coos and smiles become more frequent as the infant moves into the second half of the first year, but the first year is still a period in which infants take more than they give.

STATUS

Demands on the worker with infants are many and great. In the recent past, the infant caregiver has not enjoyed the high status associated with teaching older children. This trend is changing as researchers find more evidence that describes infant learning potential. The status of infant caregivers is rising and it will continue to rise as the quality of the day care offered becomes obvious to the general public.

Glossary

Attachment   Tendency of the young to seek to be near the chief caregiver and a few others.

Babbling   A wide range of noncrying sounds produced by infants. These begin at four to six months, and are produced most frequently during the second half of the first year.

Cooing   A limited variety of noncrying sounds produced by infants. These are produced most frequently before infants are able to sit up.

Ethology   Science of animal behavior.

Infancy   The age range from birth to one year of age.

Kinesthetic sense   Individual's awareness of the position of the body in space.

Landmarks of development   The physical characteristics or behavior that may be expected of certain age levels. Because of individual differences in development these landmarks may not appear at the indicated times.

Mobile   Hanging objects that move with air currents. Mobiles are very attractive to infants and might be hung over play yards and changing tables.

Modeling   Learning a behavior by observing another's performance of that behavior.

Passive vocabulary   Words understood but not used in speech.

Play yard   Fenced equipment to keep infant in a specific area, frequently referred to as a play pen.

Redirection   Suggesting or insisting on a change in behavior, usually in a situation where an adult is helping a child change from unacceptable to more acceptable behavior.

Reflex   Automatic response to certain stimuli.

Reinforcement   Social or material reward for a particular behavior. Reinforcement increases the probability that the reinforced behavior will occur again.

Rooting reflex   The automatic response of infants when their cheek is stroked of turning their heads and sucking.

Self-demand schedule   Arranging opportunity for feeding and sleeping according to the infant's observed need.

Separation anxiety   Emotional response of infant to separation from mother or caretaker.

Stranger anxiety   Fear of strange persons or places.

Visual accommodation   Automatic adjustment of the eye for seeing different distances.

Study Questions

1. Describe what seem to you important landmarks of development during the first month, two to three months, four to six months, seven to nine months, and ten to twelve months.
2. Outline questions you would ask yourself in selecting toys and activities for a particular infant.
3. Observe a four- to six-month-old infant and a ten- to twelve-month-old infant and compare with expectations for language described in this chapter.
4. Show how an understanding of attachment, stranger anxiety, and separation anxiety influences planning for admission and care of infants in a center.
5. Invite two parents of infants of similar age to discuss eating and sleeping patterns of their children.
6. Show how the care and guidance of infants influence their developing sense of trust.
7. Outline what you consider the most important characteristics of a worker in an infant center.

Notes

1. C. M. Drillien, "Growth and Development in a Group of Children of Very Low Birthweight," *Archives of Diseases in Childhood,* 33, 1958, p. 18.
2. K. C. Pratt, "The Neonate," in *Manual of Child Psychology,* ed. L. Carmichael, Wiley, New York, 1954, pp. 203–226.
3. W. Kessen, M. M. Haith, and P. Salapatek, "Infancy," in *Carmichael's Manual of Child Psychology,* ed. P. H. Mussen, Vol. I., 3rd ed., Wiley, New York, 1970, p. 348.
4. R. L. Fantz, "Visual Perception from Birth as Shown by Pattern Selectivity," in *Annals of New York Academy of Science,* 118, 1965, p. 801.
5. Kessen et al., 352.

6. M. M. Haith, "The Response of the Human New-born to Visual Movement," *Journal of Experimental Child Psychology,* 3, 1966, p. 242.

7. Kessen et al., p. 357.

8. A. B. Horowitz, "Habituation and Memory: Infant Cardiac Responses to Familiar and Discrepant Auditory Stimuli," *Child Development,* 43, 1972, p. 52.

9. Kessen et al., p. 321.

10. B. L. White and P. W. Castle, "Visual Exploratory Behavior Following Postnatal Handling of Infants," *Perceptual Motor Skills,* 18, 1964, p. 502; L. Casler, "The Effects of Extra Tactile Stimulation on a Group of Institutionalized Infants," *Genetic Psychology Monographs,* 71, 1965, p. 154.

11. E. B. Evans and G. E. Saia, *Day Care for Infants,* Beacon Press, Boston, 1972, pp. 193–205.

12. D. Kunnardt, *Pat the Bunny,* Western Publishing, New York, 1968.

13. D. McNeill, "The Development of Language," in *Carmichael's Manual of Child Psychology,* ed. P. Mussen, I, 3rd ed., Wiley, New York, 1970, p. 1131.

14. *Ibid.*

15. O. H. Mower, *Learning Theory and the Symbolic Processes,* Wiley, New York, 1960, p. 84.

16. E. H. Lenneberg, "Speech as a Motor Skill with Special Reference to Monaphasic Disorders," in *The Acquisition of Language,* ed., U. Bellugi and R. Brown, Monograph for Society of Research in Child Development, 29 (Serial Number 92), 1964, p. 120.

17. H. Rheingold, J. L. Gewirtz, and H. Ross. "Social Conditioning of Vocalization in the Infant," *Journal of Comparative and Physiological Psychology,* 52, 1959, p. 73.

18. H. R. Schaffer and P. E. Emerson, *The Development of Social Attachments In Infancy,* Monograph of the Society for Research in Child Development, 29 (Serial No. 94), 1964, pp. 67–68.

19. E. E. Maccoby and S. S. Feldman, *Mother-Attachment and Stranger-Reactions in the Third Year of Life,* Mono-

graph of the Society for Research in Child Development, 37 (Serial No. 146), 1972, p. 60.

20. Schaffer and Emerson, p. 21.

21. L. Casler, *Maternal Deprivation: A Critical Review of the Literature*, Monograph of the Society for Research in Child Development, 26 (Serial No. 80), 1961, p. 49.

22. Maccoby and Feldman, p. 79.

23. B. M. Caldwell, C. M. Wright, et al. "Infant Day Care and Attachment, *American Journal of Orthopsychiatry*, 40, 1970, p. 411.

24. G. Klackenberg, "Thumbsucking Frequency and Etiology," *Pediatrics*, 4, 1949, pp. 4, 420–421.

25. J. Kagan, *Change and Continuity in Infancy*, Wiley, New York, 1971, p. 188.

26. S. M. Bell and M. D. Salter Ainsworth, "Infant Crying and Maternal Responsiveness," *Child Development*, 43, 1972, p. 1179.

Supplementary Readings

Gordon, I., and R. Lally. *Baby Learning Through Baby Play*. St. Martin's Press. New York, 1970.

Painter, G. *Teach Your Baby*. Simon & Schuster, New York, 1971.

Mussen, P., J. J. Conver, and J. Kagan. *Child Development and Personality*, 4th ed. Harper & Row, New York, 1974.

Stone, L. J., and J. Church. *Childhood and Adolescence*, 3rd ed. Random House, New York, 1973.

The Toddler's Body, Language, and Thought

After reading this chapter, you should be able to:

1. predict the behavior you might expect in eighteen-, twenty-four-, and thirty-month-old children
2. outline suggestions for guiding toddlers in routines of eating, sleeping, and eliminating
3. describe ways in which adults can encourage toddlers in their desire and ability to communicate
4. describe ways to encourage toddlers' ability to think
5. describe characteristic play behavior of this period
6. describe ways adults can encourage toddlers in the development of curiosity

In this book, the period of toddlerhood is considered to be from twelve to thirty months of age. By twelve months, most babies have learned some form of locomotion, usually walking, and thus they usually are called toddlers. By thirty months, toddlers have acquired enough autonomy, socialization, and skills to move them into the realm of the preschool child. Of course, any definition by months is artificial because of the wide range in rate of individual development and is done only for the convenience of the authors and readers.

Table 2 is given here for your convenience, as a reference when thinking about physical, motor, language, and social development. It gives the landmark achievements, and is intended only as a guideline for your observations of toddlers. It is *not* intended for use in comparing or evaluating particular children because children's individual differences vary widely at all ages.

Landmarks of Development

Renaissance paintings portray toddlers as cherubim and cupids, but that is too serene to be accurate. Perhaps comedian Bill Cosby gave a more realistic picture: "Give me two hundred active two-year-olds and I can conquer the world." Actually, describing toddlers is difficult. If you have not had contact with any, words could never adequately prepare you for the experience. And if you have been exposed to them, words could never accurately describe it. With this in mind, we present the characteristics of the toddler.

ONE TO ONE AND ONE-HALF YEARS

Toddlers still have the physical appearance of babies. Their stomachs protrude and their arms seem to stick out from their bodies. They walk stiffly, with their feet wide apart. Their energy seems endless—they climb on, push, pull, pound, open, close, and throw objects. They can sit in child-size chairs, but their aim for getting into them is only fairly accurate.

Their hand development is much improved over infants'. They can pick up and release some objects. By the end of this period they can build two- to three-cube towers and can make random marks with crayons on paper.

TABLE 2 *Landmarks of Toddlerhood Development*

PHYSICAL, MOTOR, AND LANGUAGE DEVELOPMENT	SOCIAL DEVELOPMENT
1–1½ years	
Walks (10–20 months)	May be upset when separated from mother
Sits on chair with fair aim	
Builds 2–3 cube tower	Obeys limited commands
Makes lines on paper with crayon	Makes no attempt at communicating information
Has definite repertoire of words— more than 3 and less than 50	Shows no frustration at not being understood
Progresses rapidly with understanding vocabulary	
1½–2 years	
Runs, kicks a ball	Temper tantrums (1–3 years)
May be capable of bowel and bladder control	Frequently does opposite of what is told
Has vocabulary of more than 200 words	Displays increased interest in communicating with others
Size at 2 years: 23–30 pounds, 32–35 inches	
2–2½ years	
Jumps into air with both feet	Shows frustration if not understood by adults
Takes a few steps on tiptoe	
Can move fingers independently	Imitates parents' actions
Uses 2- to 5-word sentences	Displays interest in other children
	Engages in brief periods of parallel play

SOURCE: Adapted from Boyd R. McCandless and Ellis Evans, *Children and Youth: Psychosocial Development,* Dryden Press, Hinsdale, Illinois, 1973, p. 13, and Charles P. Smith, *Child Development,* William C. Brown, New York, 1966, pp. 8–9. Reprinted by permission of Dryden Press and Charles P. Smith.

Mealtime is fun but messy. Usually toddlers can feed themselves with some accuracy with a spoon, although they may need help, particularly at the end of the meal as they tire. They can drink from cups but enjoy pouring the milk into their food.

Their vocabularies are increasing and although they may not speak many words, their understanding vocabularies are growing rapidly. They are able to respond to simple verbal directions and commands. They show little or no frustration at not having their vocalizations understood by adults.

Socially they are interested in their environment and want to explore it all. They like to listen to music and seem to have a built-in sense of rhythm for dancing. Looking at books or at themselves in a mirror are favorite activities, although their attention span is short and they change activities frequently. They may become upset when separated from their mothers or fathers and alternate between clinging to them and leaving them to explore their surroundings. This is a sign of attachment, discussed in Chapter 2.

ONE AND ONE-HALF TO TWO YEARS

Well established in toddlerhood, children of this age are secure on their feet while walking and can even run without falling. As they run, their bodies lean forward. They can walk upstairs but do not alternate feet. At the beginning of this period, they usually go down stairs by sitting and bumping their way down or reverting to all fours to creep down backward. By the end of this period, they are usually able to walk down stairs without alternating feet, and can kick a ball.

Their hand development is improving and they can turn a doorknob, which often opens new areas for exploration. They can make a vertical mark with a crayon on paper although they still make random marks. In addition to the two- or three-block towers of the pre-

ceeding period, toddlers of this age are capable of building three-block towers or horizontal walls. They like playing with the cubes and especially seem to enjoy toys they can manipulate, take apart, and put together again. *Nesting toys* (objects that fit inside each other) are particularly good at this stage of eye-hand coordination.

Mealtime continues to be messy as toddlers mix and stir their food together. They drink well from cups and handle spoons better than they did previously, although much feeding is still done with the fingers.

Vocabularies continue to expand rapidly and may consist of over two hundred words. These children are able to name most of the items in their environment. They seem particularly interested in communication and may produce two-word phrases that help their efforts to be understood. As their vocabularies increase, they may be able to tell you when they have to go to the toilet and may be capable of bowel and bladder control during their waking hours.

Socially, they are into everything but their attention span is still relatively short. Toward the end of this period, they imitate games and actions of adults and older children although they are still too egocentric to play with other children. They engage in *solitary* or *parallel play*, which will be discussed later in this chapter. They are not capable of sharing. Although they can follow directions and simple commands, they often do exactly the opposite of what they are told to do. Temper tantrums show toddlers' frustration at not being able to do things just their way.

TWO TO TWO AND ONE-HALF YEARS

Older toddlers have greatly improved their physical coordination. They walk almost completely erect and their stomachs do not protrude as they did at twelve and eighteen months of age. They jump into the air with both feet, stand briefly on one foot, take a few steps on tip toes, and jump from a chair or stool.

They have good hand and finger coordination and can move their fingers independently. Their manipulation of objects is much improved and they can pick up and release very small objects. They can make horizontal marks with crayons on paper. By the end of this period, they may be able to combine the horizontal and vertical block building with some evidence of awareness of balance.[1]

TWO AND ONE-HALF TO THREE YEARS

Language development progresses rapidly during this stage and toddlers add new words to their vocabularies almost daily. Babbling has almost completely disappeared; they are intent upon communication. They become very frustrated when they are not understood by adults. Single-word utterances of early toddlerhood have been almost completely replaced by two- to five-word phrases and sentences. They seem to understand most of what is said to them.

Their social development has also progressed rapidly. They do more imitating of adults and older children than they did previously and also show greater interest in children of the same age level. Frequently they engage in brief periods of parallel play but they are still not able to share. "It's mine," dominates their approach to play. Books, poems, nursery rhymes, records, puzzles, manipulative toys, dolls and doll furniture, blocks, and wheel toys all interest them.

They are still very dependent on adults but their sense of autonomy is growing stronger and they want to do things for and by themselves. As they develop from infancy, through toddlerhood, and into preschool-age children, they experience rapid changes. Being aware of these changes will help you meet the special needs that they create for toddlers.

Guidance for Physical Growth

During toddlerhood many changes occur within the toddlers' bodies and in their daily routines. As their caregiver, you will be concerned with meeting their needs relating to nutrition, resting in groups, and toilet training.

NUTRITION

Nutrition is extremely important to the growth and development of all young children. You have just read the characteristics of toddlers. Their energy is boundless and their curiosity is fostered by their ability to explore. Only if they are properly fed and nourished can they progress on a healthy basis. The quality and quantity of their food is important. The National Research Council recommends 1100 calories for children one to two years of age and 1250 calories for children from two to three years of age.[2] A large portion of these calories should be in the form of protein, which is needed for the rapid growth of muscles.

Decreasing quantity of food. Physical growth proceeds more slowly during toddlerhood than during infancy. During toddlerhood, children will grow four to five inches and gain four to five pounds. As indicated in Table 2, two-year-olds are usually thirty-two to thirty-five inches tall and weigh twenty-three to thirty pounds. As this growth rate levels off, toddlers require less food and their appetites decline sharply. You should not be upset by a decrease in food intake. Give toddlers opportunities to choose from a well-balanced diet and, as with children of all ages, do not use pressure or continuous urging to force them to eat. Forcing may create a feeding problem as they continue to refuse the food.

Accepting solid food and weaning. You may be able to increase solid food intake by decreasing the milk intake. Milk consumed early in a meal gives toddlers a full feeling and decreases their appetite for solid food. Gradual weaning from the bottle to the cup, which is given along with and following the meal, may help alter this feeding situation.

Before attempting to wean toddlers from their bottles, parents must be consulted. As was mentioned in the last chapter, parents have the right to decide when their children will begin a new process such as being fed solid food or weaned from a bottle. Parents and staff working together will provide consistency in toddlers' daily home and center routines.

After the decision to wean has been made, proceed slowly. Infants who began drinking daily from a cup or glass at five to six months may be ready at twelve to fifteen months to give up the bottle completely. But they *may* not be ready for another year. Let the children and their parents guide you. A struggle over the bottle may make them refuse to drink from a glass for several months. Strive to make mealtime a happy time, not a time for battling.

Developing skills in self-feeding. Mealtime can be fun. When toddlers feel their food, they enjoy the feeding process, and should be permitted to finger their vegetables and squeeze their cereal. And, as much as possible, let them learn to feed themselves. Children learn by experimenting and practicing. Most toddlers can effectively handle a spoon and fork by fifteen months if during the preceding months they have been allowed to practice spoon and finger feeding. Often the long delay in self-feeding is caused by lack of patience in adults who find it neater, faster, and more efficient to do the spoon feeding themselves. When toddlers are capable of getting even the tiniest amount of food on the spoon and into their mouths, they should be allowed and encouraged to feed themselves. Showing them how much better you can do it for them will only discourage them.

One sixteen-month-old toddler strongly resisted his mother's attempts to feed him. She wanted to make sure he ate the food he needed; he wanted to feed himself. She wanted to avoid a messy floor and high chair; he wanted to feed himself. She wanted to hurry and get mealtime over as quickly as possible; he wanted to feed himself. Every time she offered him a spoonful of food, he shook his head, waved his hands, and screamed, "No, not me! No, not me! No! No! No!" He wanted to feed himself. When his mother acknowledged his request and handed him a spoon, he happily played in his food and eventually fed himself. Children must be allowed to mature gradually in this area.

RESTING IN GROUPS

A second area of concern to the day care staff is naptime. Some toddlers may not require exactly the same length of time for rest or nap as others, but as a general guide, the staff should know that most toddlers need approximately twelve hours of sleep at night plus one to three hours daily in naps. This may cause some difficulties at the center, for it is impossible to regulate toddlers to sleep at the same time and for the same length of time. All children operate on their own individual schedules, which agree with their families' schedules. Toddlers who are awakened at 6:30 and brought to the center by 7:30, so their parents can be at work at 8:00, will be on a different schedule than toddlers who sleep until 8:30 and come to the center at 9:00.

Some toddlers require a morning nap or rest period in their cribs or with quiet activities. Others will want to nap for one to three hours after lunch. They may also rearrange their schedules from one day to the next, due to changes in their personal situations.

Signs of fatigue. The day care worker must be particularly alert to sleep needs. Many children give obvious signs of being ready to rest. When one toddler becomes tired, he starts to sing a one-syllable repetition of "ah-ah-ah-ah." Another picks up her "scratchy" (blanket) and carries it around with her. Another requests his "paci" (pacifier). Another rubs her eyes and stares into space. Still another plays until the very last minute, when his head gradually falls over his toys and he is asleep. When you see and recognize these individual signs that say, "I'm ready for a rest," you can guide the children to their cribs.

This is not to suggest that toddlers can be permitted to be the sole judges of the amount of time required for their rest. They may stubbornly refuse to sleep even though their eyelids droop and they grow cross and irritable. At these times, the worker must patiently but firmly insist that they rest. Often a few minutes of quiet rocking or a musical animal will provide the quiet and reassurance needed for toddlers to drift off into a well-deserved rest. Although an ideal nap room provides a quiet, darkened spot for rest, children may become accustomed to sleeping in noisy rooms as well. A screen or curtain to block off the vision of the about-to-nap children may be all that is necessary.

Adjusting to individual needs.   Both staff and children must adjust to the group's schedule, and eating in a group provides a valuable experience for toddlers: therefore, children should not consistently miss scheduled meal- and naptimes. Major consideration must be given, however, to the children's needs. If this means that occasionally some children must eat their lunches at 11:30 instead of 12:00 because they are too tired to wait, teachers can often rearrange their schedules. Although it is inconvenient, it is much easier for the staff to be flexible than it is for toddlers to comply with rigid rules that allow no exceptions.

TOILET TRAINING

Much has been written on a third area involved in meeting the needs of toddlers: toilet training. Because of its impact on children's development, the importance of

this subject cannot and must not be overlooked. Toilet training is a crucial area for children and the adults who care for them.

It is quite understandable that you will be anxious to train all toddlers as early as possible. However, this important beginning time will be different for individual children, and it should be decided by parents when they feel their children are ready to begin. Usually children begin to show some signs of readiness during the second half of the second year and have developed language to the extent that they can tell you when they need to go to the toilet.

Remember that, since birth, the bladder and intestine have emptied automatically. Now adults are encouraging and even expecting children to control these previously automatic responses. The amount of difficulty children have in learning this control may be very dependent upon adults' attitudes toward toddlers and their efforts.

"Broken" children. A generation ago, toilet training was a harsh, unpleasant ordeal to be endured by parents and children, in which parents attempted to "break" their children as quickly as possible, preferably by ten to fifteen months of age. Great status and praise were given to mothers who trained their children by the time they were a year old. Usually this was accomplished by forcing toddlers to spend long periods of time on the toilet seat or potty chair and spanking, scolding, and shaming them for accidents. Unfortunately, this method often "broke" children's sense of autonomy and feelings of self-worth, in addition to breaking them from wetting and soiling their diapers.

Many of today's mothers and day care workers are just as preoccupied with training as were their own mothers. A librarian reported that a mother with a thirteen-month-old child checked out a book that claimed to tell the mother how to train her child in one day. The librarian added that the mother had renewed the book three times. Perhaps a healthier attitude is represented in a father's comment: "I estimate that my wife or I have changed our baby two thousand six hundred forty-seven times in the sixteen months since his birth. What difference will a few more diapers make? We're not in a hurry. We're looking for a better way to train than the way we were trained."

Effective training procedure. Perhaps a better way to train children is to wait until they show signs of readiness, such as regularity of bowel movements, awareness of being the cause of a soiled diaper, and sufficient language to communicate their need to use the toilet. Proceed slowly. Encourage them. Show praise for success today (although not exaggerated praise) and optimism for tomorrow. Be casual and calm. Avoid pressure and punishment.

Toilet training, like the learning of all skills, is a gradual process; it is not something that can be accomplished in a few days. It may take months. Many children are not completely trained, day and night, until they are three years old or older. If at any time during the training process children rebel and resist going to the bathroom or sitting on the potty or toilet, ease up. Do not force them. Wait until they are ready to try again. Do not make them lose face. Remember, the goal is to break their urinating and defecating in their diapers, not to break their wills.

One mother who was expecting her second child decided to train her fifteen-month-old son before the new baby arrived. She began with a very positive attitude, asking if he had to go to the potty. While there, she read to him, played games with him, and generally entertained him. He apparently thought the attention was great, but he didn't wet in the potty. Soon he began to resent her asking (nagging) him about having to go to the potty. He resisted sitting on the chair. Often she would force him to sit for twenty to thirty minutes, and as soon as he got up, he would wet on the floor. When she asked if he had to go to the potty, he would scream, "No! No! No!" She put the potty chair away and waited. At twenty months he began asking to go to the potty and his mother could respond to his request. He was ready for toilet training.

Consider toilet training a maturational process through which all children pass, not a traumatic battle of wills between toddlers and trainers. Do not create a situation that is bound to bring negative feelings into the close adult-child relationship. Proceed in a matter-of-fact, warm, positive manner. When overwhelmed by the hundreds of diapers per child, remember this is a part of the child-care process.

Trained toddlers. A teacher in the infant toddler section of a large day care center mentioned that she often had mixed feelings when toddlers became toilet trained. "When you care for a baby every day, you get very attached to each other. Diaper-changing time has always been a special time of communication for me and my babies. We laugh and play and talk together. I pat and love them and always get and give a special little hug at the end of each change as I lift them down to the floor. Toilet training is somewhat of a separation process. They are more independent—they are growing up and they grow up so very fast. It's not the wet and soiled diapers I miss, you understand, it's the time we spend together. When a toddler is trained, I have to look for other times for us to communicate with each other."

Accidents. Of course, accidents will happen after children appear to have control over elimination. Be patient. Look for causes. Have the toddlers been embarrassed, humiliated, or shamed? Has the family undergone a change? Is a new baby on the way? Are toddlers cutting teeth or reacting to medication? Did a pet die? Expect regression, especially in young toddlers. Accept it. Do not dwell on it. And do not punish for it.

The time babies spend in diapers is relatively short.

When the soiled diapers are gone, make sure no soiled memories remain of harsh, punitive toilet-training procedures. You will find such negative training procedures unnecessary if you will wait until toddlers show they are physically mature enough to be trained. In addition to improved communication skills, they must be able to control bowel and bladder muscles. This requires development of considerable motor skills.

Development of Motor Skills

As you noted in studying the characteristics of toddlers and the landmarks table 2, coordination of *gross* and *fine motor skills* develop rapidly during the twelve- through thirty-month age period. Adults can provide the play materials and an environment in which this development will be encouraged.

At the beginning of toddlerhood, some children are able to walk only with support, if at all. Soon they acquire enough balance to walk, run, climb into and out of boxes, beds, etc., clamber up and down, jump, stand on one foot, and walk on tiptoes. These are *gross motor skills*.

Fine motor skills, such as hand coordination, are also improving. At the beginning of toddlerhood, many children cannot release an object they have picked up. Gradually toddlers learn to pick up, release, and throw items, make random horizontal and vertical crayon marks, skillfully use a spoon, fork, cup, and small glass, and help in dressing and undressing themselves, including zipping, buttoning, and snapping.

Motor development can be fostered by providing toddlers with suitable toys and equipment, which can be made or purchased by the day care center. Expensive materials are not necessary, but some specific types should be available for developing gross and fine motor skills.

Just as infants are attracted by moving objects, toddlers also are interested in movement. Push toys and pull toys are particularly important, because many of them provide double movement. This allows children to focus on objects and listen to sounds while practicing motor skills. The corn popper is an example; as toddlers push the toy, little balls bounce up and down inside the clear plastic dome.

Push toys seem to be more satisfactory then pull toys. Toddlers cannot get full enjoyment from pull toys unless someone else pulls for them, or unless they can walk backward as they pull the toys themselves and watch their movements. Since most children of this age are not experienced walkers, proceeding backward does not seem to fit their capabilities. Also, the string on pull toys seems to encourage older toddlers to swing them in the air, which is very dangerous in a group of young children.

Large cardboard boxes with holes cut for climbing in and out provide experiences for body movement and exploration in space. Steps for climbing, low sawhorses and planks, along with sturdy low chairs or stools, also provide opportunities for improving gross motor skills.

MATERIALS TO ENCOURAGE FINE MOTOR SKILLS

As hand coordination begins to improve, manipulative materials are a necessity. Items that can be taken apart and put together provide opportunities to use the improving pincer movement. Puzzles, pots, pans, spoons, small blocks, stacking and nesting toys, large tie shoes, and dressing boards all foster development of fine-muscle control.

If toddlers are to develop motor skills, they must have the chance to use their large and small muscles. They need a safe environment that will let them explore and exercise without physical harm. The day care center can be organized to allow freedom for exploration. It is a setting created for, or at least converted to, children's need to explore. Unlike the typical home, fragile figurines, ashtrays, lamps, and knickknacks are absent. There are no stereo sets, china cabinets, silver chests, or shaky tables. Most items in the center are conducive to handling by the children, and they are at children's eye level, within reach. As they climb on and handle new objects, toddlers will develop better coordination and improved skills.

As you encourage development of gross and fine motor skills, with appropriate toys and games, you encourage their language skills through verbal interactions. Table 2 points out progress in language development.

Development of Language

The specialized cries of infants give way to the advanced communication of toddlers. Although infants' babbling included all the sounds required in any language, in toddlers those sounds that are not part of the language they hear spoken are being or have been dropped. Even the babbling sometimes sounds like a jumble of the infants' language-to-be. As toddlers acquire vocabulary, they can make their wants and needs known.

VOCABULARY

It is very difficult to make an accurate estimate of the number of words in toddlers' *active vocabulary,* or the words they are able to use in speech. Just as infants understand more than they can communicate, toddlers also understand more words than they actually use. Also, one word, such as "milk," may indicate the meaning for a whole sentence. It may mean, "I want milk,"

"Where is the milk?," "Here is the milk," "I spilled the milk," or "The cat drank the milk."

The exact size of vocabulary is not important. What *is* important is that toddlers are willing and able to communicate. You can help them to improve their ability to make themselves understood by helping them add to their vocabularies.

IMITATION AND REINFORCEMENT

The processes of imitation and reinforcement seem to influence language development in toddlers. As younger toddlers babble, they make some utterances that sound like adult speech. These sounds are immediately rewarded or reinforced by parents or caregivers who are eager for the children to talk. Through imitation and reinforcement, along with other methods, toddlers add to their vocabularies.

The amount and type of reinforcement you offer children will affect their rates of vocabulary development. You can help them by talking and reading to them and by labeling objects in their immediate environment. If you are helping children learn the word "chair," it will be more useful to them if they see, touch, climb on, and sit in labeled chairs, and not just see a picture of a chair. This will not always be possible and labels should not be withheld from children simply because you cannot show them the actual objects.

In addition to providing labels for items, you can also label activities. When toddlers run or fall, you can explain to them what has happened by saying, "You can run!" or, "You fell." When they are interested in a particular object, you can label the object and the children's activity with it. For example, showing children a ball, tell them to throw the ball, take the ball, kick the ball, pick the ball up, or roll the ball.

It is best, when using verbs, to use the same tense that you intend the toddlers to use, to avoid confusion. Thus, if toddlers run, say, "You can run," instead of "You are running," or "You ran." Imitating your label, they may say, "run" or, as they develop further, they may state, "Me run."

PHRASES AND SENTENCES

At approximately eighteen months, toddlers begin to put together words to form phrases and sentences. Although their first phrases are usually direct imitations of what they have heard spoken, they soon combine words that they have not heard spoken together.

Like their single-word utterances, their phrases may indicate meaning for a whole sentence. "Bye-bye mama," may have several meanings—it may mean, "Mother is going out," "Mother has gone out," "I want Mother to go out," "I want to go out," "I want Mother to take me out." Or it may have a completely different meaning to the individual toddlers who construct the phrase.

INTERPRETING MEANING

It may be difficult to figure out the exact meaning of toddlers' utterances because you cannot understand their words or because they do not understand their own words. Toddlers sometimes become confused between the meaning and the use of specific words. They have the right idea, but use the wrong words.

A two-year-old provided us with the following examples of word confusion that could have led to misunderstanding between adult and child. At various times, Sarah announced that her baby brother John had a frog on his nose (meaning a bug), that John was broken (asleep, not moving), that she wanted sugar on her potatoes (salt), and that her plastic cup was broken and she wanted her mother to sew it up (glue or fix it). She also stated that she wanted shampoo in her bath water (bubbles), that in a passing car she saw a lion (dog), that she ate a stick (pretzel), that her friend tried to bite her (yawned), that she wanted rope for her hair (ribbons), that her horse was eating John (wooden riding horse had fallen on the baby), that her tummy fell out (she spit up), and that Jenni flew away (her doll fell off the porch railing).

Toddlers also often make mistakes regarding relationships with people, numbers, and time. The general terms showing relationship often confuse toddlers. They may have difficulty understanding that their mothers call someone else "mother" and that their friends all have mothers, too. Toddlers often call several caregivers by the term "mother" and may refer to their own parents by their first names. The fact that relatives are not easily substituted for or replaced may be a concern. One toddler whose father had been out of town for several weeks suggested that she and her mother go to the store and buy a new daddy.

Numbers and time, although occasionally used correctly, generally are not understood by toddlers. They may count to five, ten, or twenty, but do so by memorization without recognizing a one-to-one correspondence and may substitute a new number at any time. Such time concepts as tomorrow, yesterday, this afternoon, next week, soon, in a few minutes, and a long time ago may have little meaning. Toddlers may use the terms randomly and interchangeably. One toddler stated that he heard a train. His mother replied that she heard it, too. He then insisted that he heard it two, three, five, seven! And added that yesterday he would go see the train, in five more minutes.

Adults are accustomed to factual statements and generally accept what they hear as being accurate. However, since toddlers sometimes use the wrong word, or do not understand the words they use, it is often difficult to find their meaning while they are in the process of developing more precise and accurate language.

You can help toddlers in their language development in many ways. Possibly the most important ways are to talk, listen, and read to them.

Toddlers usually like being talked to and respond with enthusiasm. Sometimes they overdo it and try to dominate all conversation. One mother reported that her two-year-old son interrupted talk directed to anyone but him. He often stated, "Stop! Don't talk! Don't talk! Talk to me!"

As with infants, a one-to-one dialogue is important to toddlers' speech development because children model the speech of those adults with whom they have a close relationship. Taking time to talk with toddlers and encourage them through reinforcement to imitate your labels of items and actions contributes to their language development.

A second way to encourage them is to respond to their vocalizations and actions. Listen to them. Let them be the initiators and you be the listener, the resource person. You need not always respond with lengthy answers or explanations; sometimes a one- or two-word response will be all they need to encourage them to continue their own vocalizations. It is very important, however, that you try to understand their words and meaning. If you do not understand, listen more carefully. Do not shake your head and say, "Yes, that's fine," when you do not know what they are saying. Making themselves understood is very important to toddlers. As their vocabularies grow, it will be easier for them to communicate.

A third way to improve communication skills is through daily exposure to books. Books must have sturdy pages, firm bindings, and plenty of bright, colorful pictures. Toddlers seem to enjoy having access to books they can "read" to themselves. They also benefit from having an adult read to them. One study reports on parents who read for ten to fifteen minutes a day to their one-year-old babies. At twenty months of age, their children were able to comprehend more words than children in a matched control group who had not been read to daily.[3]

Toddlers who bring books to the teacher and demand, "you read," probably will listen to several books. However, reading sessions should be broken up with active play periods. Children never should be forced to sit still and listen for longer than they can comfortably pay attention. If they become restless or uninterested, they should be permitted to get up and leave, even in the middle of a story. Forcing children to stay when they are tired or bored may create negative feelings associated with books.

As you read to the interested children, do not forget the little girl in the blocks corner or the quiet boy in the play house. They also need to be encouraged to develop an interest in books. They need time for talking, listening, holding, and general communicating, too. The busy caregiver may tend to forget the nontalkers, who may talk less and less because they are not encouraged.

Motivating language development will help toddlers in their efforts to master the complex process of communication and thus progress in intellectual development.

Development of Thought

In adults, language and thought are closely related, but their relation in young children is unclear. We know that words express thought, but there is some question as to whether or not thought is possible without language.

THOUGHT WITHOUT LANGUAGE

Jean Piaget has studied the intellectual development of children and can provide much insight about thought without language. According to Piaget, young toddlers are in the sensorimotor period from birth to two years.[4]

They can accomplish simple tasks by means of mental images, without the aid of language. Toddlers who have acquired object permanence and search for a ball that has rolled behind another toy are showing evidence of thinking without speaking. Older toddlers have progressed to the preoperational stage.

Two to seven years. During this stage, toddlers gradually acquire language, have dreams, and engage in symbolic play, which will be discussed in the following section.

Children develop and express their thinking through various kinds of play. Young toddlers' play usually takes the form of *solitary play*. As they progress through toddlerhood, they also participate in *onlooker*, *parallel*, and *cooperative play*.

Solitary play. Toddlers spend much of the day in solitary play, in which they do their own thing, often oblivious to the presence of others. Through solitary dramatic play they learn things about themselves that no one can teach them. As they develop a better understanding of their capabilities and limitations, they gain self-confidence, increase their sense of autonomy, and form a more realistic self-concept. Apparently, as they work out a better understanding of who they are, they become more interested in others.

Onlooker play. Although they do not actually participate in the activities of others, toddlers show definite interest in them through onlooker play. One two-year-old watched two older toddlers engaged in a game of ring-around-the-rosy. She obviously enjoyed their merriment. She laughed, wiggled, and danced as she stared at them. Finally, when they fell down, she fell down. When the caregiver asked the toddler to join the children, she refused. Watching was fun, but participating was a little too threatening. She enjoyed observing and copying behavior but she was not sure she actually wanted to join the group activity.

Parallel play. Still not ready for group play, two individual toddlers may engage in parallel play, staying close
together, busy with the same type of activity, yet not
communicating or playing with each other. An example
of this may be two children sitting in a sand box, each
with shovel, pail, and sifter. They are near each other
but not actively involved with each other. Toddlers often
participate in parallel play, but this type of play is not
exclusively characteristic to this age group and will occur
far into the preschool years. Often even their language
is a parallel conversation in which the two children talk
about unrelated issues, not really discussing them with
each other, but rather just throwing out their comments
to anyone who hears.

Cooperative play. Older toddlers may spend short
periods of the day in cooperative play, during which two
or more children coordinate their activities and actually
play with each other. The two toddlers who played separately in the sand box may play together by having one
hold a pail while the other fills it with sand. Or, two
toddlers in the blocks may combine their block supplies
to build one long road.

It is usually during cooperative play periods that we
see symbolic or dramatic play, but this type of play is also
evident in the other forms of play.

Symbolic play. We mentioned that during the preoperational stage, toddlers engage in symbolic play. In symbolic (also called dramatic) play, they treat objects as if
they were something else and act out familiar happenings. This type of play becomes more popular as the
children's imaginations develop and they can re-enact
more scenes. The most popular subjects for dramatic
play are those with which the children are most familiar.
Typically seen in dramatic play are such routine happenings as eating, dressing, bathing, getting into bed,
picking up toys, talking on the telephone, watching the
mail carrier come and go, swinging, climbing stairs,
taking a walk, riding in the car, and feeding the baby.

Observing children involved in dramatic play gives
the teacher insight into their feelings. Often they will act
out scenes, not as they actually have happened, but as
they perceived them. Twenty-month-old Sarah was bathing her doll while her mother bathed Sarah's baby
brother. When the baby slipped from the mother's hand
and fell into the tub, Sarah threw her doll in her pan of
water and announced, "Baby all gone." Perhaps Sarah
thought her mother intentionally dropped the baby and
therefore did the same thing with her doll. Or perhaps
Sarah wished that her baby brother would actually go
away and was acting out her own negative feelings toward her sibling.

Dramatic play provides many opportunities for expressing all kinds of feelings, including hostility. It also
provides avenues for exploration and encourages
toddlers' curiosity.

Toddlers are curious by nature. They are so curious and so energetic that many people who are unaccustomed to being around toddlers, think they are hyperactive. This characteristic should be encouraged, however, not discouraged, because curiosity promotes learning.

Toddlers spend much of their time learning through looking. One study observed that staring and thereby gaining information was the most frequent activity of one- to three-year-old children.[5] They also spend considerable time conducting simple experiments, which often occur during mealtime. One particular toddler seemed to be studying the concept of buoyancy as he dropped a pea into his juice cup. Later in the meal, he seemed fascinated with removing ice cubes from his drink and watching them melt away on his high chair tray. He went on doing this until all the food was gone.

Toddlers develop intellectually by such experimenting and by exploring. Explorations provide new experiences, which lead to questions and answers with exchanges of new information. Eighteen-month-old Patty opened a cabinet door and found a box, which she also opened. Inside the box was an object with several buttons. She pushed a button; nothing happened. She pushed another button; still nothing happened. She pushed three more buttons and a bell rang, a drawer opened, and little number popped up inside a glass window. She had discovered how a toy cash register works and she was delighted. Her explorations opened many areas of conversation for her and her teacher.

When Patty discovered the toy cash register, she was playing, but the experience, with her teacher's interest, encouraged her thinking. Such intellectual development is of utmost importance during toddlerhood. Adults must be alert and encourage thinking by providing rich play experiences.

Rich play experiences. Do not let the word "rich" upset you—most rich play experiences cost nothing in terms of dollars and cents. A university-affiliated day care center was closing for the summer when a mother came to talk with the head teacher. "I'm worried about how the summer will affect my child. She has almost no toys at home and will miss the center so much," she reported. The teacher's reply was, "Yes, I understand, but she has you."

As we have mentioned, toddlers can now make an object into something else through symbolic play. Their imaginations are developing, and you can help. Provide a cardboard box that can be used as a boat and a log that serves as a train. Discarded draperies and bedding can turn a play yard into a hundred exciting experiences. A box of cotton makes a snowy day setting for dolls and toy animals. A pair of socks and scraps of yarn become friendly puppets, and a sheet draped over a card table makes a house or a hiding place. Other equipment suggestions were listed in the section on motor development earlier in this chapter.

Expensive toys are not necessary, but a variety of basic play materials is essential for fostering intellectual development. Toddlers want to discover all that awaits them. They are interested in manipulative toys. They enjoy climbing on everything from blocks to a deluxe outdoor climber. They climb the stairs and go down the slide by themselves (although they may become frightened when they get to the top). The sandbox and water table teach concepts of texture, quantity, and space.

Carrying things, big and small, is a favorite activity, and may be accompanied by "Me do it, me do it, me do it . . . too heavy, you do it." Often it seems that the process of moving objects from one place to another is more important than the finished arrangement. We observed a nineteen-month-old toddler moving a pile of nine small square blocks from a box to a nearby table. Although she could easily have carried two or more blocks at a time, she joyfully made nine trips, taking one block at a time. This also shows toddlers' inability to plan and look ahead.

During quieter play periods, toddlers enjoy looking at books and having someone read to them. If no adult is available, they may very well read the story aloud in their own personal, nonintelligible gibberish. Puzzles with limited numbers of large pieces are also favorite toys that encourage thinking. Adults often are amazed at toddlers' skill in working complex puzzles. Children repeatedly choose puzzles designed as nursery rhymes. They learn to enjoy the rhymes and simple songs.

Guidance. The adult caregiver who talks to children is far more important than equipment or materials used in encouraging thinking and curiosity. An available adult can encourage explorations and offer explanations as children go along. As a caregiver, you can indicate to toddlers that thinking can be fun and you can play along with their games. A bright-eyed two-year-old made up a game that she played with her teachers. The toddler gave the command and the teacher responded. "Go to sleep (close your eyes). Wake up. Go to sleep. Wake up." She laughed as the teacher did as she commanded and she herself played along, partially closing her own eyes and opening them wide at her own instructions.

You can encourage thought-stimulating play by providing props. Toddlers seem to enjoy putting on and taking off clothes, hats, and shoes. Dolls with furniture (child size) are needed, as is an unbreakable, full-length mirror. A well-equipped play kitchen provides an ideal setting for much of the dramatic play period.

Also, if parents or teachers are available for play, toddlers still enjoy infant-type games, such as "pat-a-cake" and "peek-a-boo." While playing, they exaggerate their fear and surprise and laugh heartily at adults who encourage their clowning gestures.

Perhaps one of the most important ways to encourage thinking and curiosity is talking with children. As the responsible adult, you should answer their questions. Toddlers are notorious for their repetition of "What's that?" One adult observed that a toddler asked "What's that?" fourteen times on a twenty-minute evening walk. Each time the adult supplied the word. Ten of the fourteen times, the toddler repeated the new word as if determined to add it to her vocabulary.

As toddlers have the freedom and encouragement to explore their environments, they find that as well as being filled with things, the world is also filled with many people. With continued freedom and encouragement, they will form relationships with other children and adults.

Glossary

Active vocabulary Words understood and used in speech.

Cooperative play Two or more children playing together.

Fine motor skills Ability to coordinate small muscles of the hands.

Gross motor skills Ability to coordinate large muscles of the body.

Nesting toys Objects of graduated size that fit inside each other. These are good for developing fine motor skills.

Onlooker play Watching and enjoying the play of others.

Parallel play Playing beside, although not actually with, another child.

Solitary play Playing alone.

Stacking toys Play materials that require placing one piece on top of the other, usually with a rod to hold the pieces together.

Symbolic play Use of imagination in labeling items and acting out familiar happenings.

Toddlerhood Age range from twelve to thirty months of age.

Study Questions

1. Discuss the importance of nutrition and feeding during toddlerhood and elaborate on the problems involved.
2. Discuss toilet training procedures and their effect upon children's present and future development.
3. Observe three toddlers, one in each stage of toddlerhood, and record activities that help to develop gross and fine motor skills.
4. Talk and play with a toddler for approximately thirty minutes. Be particularly aware of the extent of vocabulary and of phrase and sentence usage. Listen for evidence of word confusion.
5. Observe a group of toddlers and record incidences involving cooperative play. How did the play begin? How long did the play last? What caused the play to end?

Notes

1. A. Gesell, F. Ilg, L. Ames and J. Rodell, *Infant and Child: In the Culture of Today*. Harper & Row, New York, 1964, p. 322.
2. H. Fleck, *Introduction to Nutrition*, 2nd ed. Macmillan, New York, 1971, p. 251.
3. O. C. Irwin, "Infant Speech Effect of Systematic Reading of Stories," *Journal of Speech and Hearing Research*, 3, 1960, p. 189.
4. D. Elkind, "Giant in the Nursery School—Jean Piaget," in *Annual Editions Readings in Human Development '73–'74*, Dushkin Publishing Group, Guilford, Conneticut, 1973, p. 9.
5. B. White, B. Kaban, J. Marmor and B. Sapiro, "Patterns of Experience During the Second and Third Years of Life: Results and Discussion," in B. White and J. Watts, *Experience and Environment*. Prentice-Hall, Englewood Cliffs, 1973, p. 90.

Supplementary Readings

Beller, E. K. "Adult-Child Interaction and Personalized Day Care." In *Day Care: Resources for Decisions*, ed., E. H. Grotberg, Office of Economic Opportunity, Washington, D.C., 1971.

Brazelton, T. B. *Toddlers and Parents*. Delacorte Press, Seymour Lawrence, New York, 1974.

Church, J. *Understanding Your Child from Birth to Three*. Random House, New York, 1973.

Cohen, M. "A Warning to Conscientious Mothers." *Today's Health Magazine*, February, 1974.

Gordon, I., B. Guinagh, and R. E. Jester. *Child Learning Through Child Play*. St. Martin's Press. New York, 1972.

Levine, C. "Why Some Preschoolers Cling to Babyish Ways." *Parent's Magazine,* November, 1972.

Petterson, C. C. *A Child Grows Up*. Alfred Publishing, New York, 1974.

Upchurch, B. *Easy To Do Toys and Activities for Infants and Toddlers*. University of North Carolina, Greensboro, 1971.

The Toddler's Relationships

After reading this chapter, you should be able to:

1. discuss expectations and adult guidance in conflicts among toddlers over play materials
2. describe ways adults can encourage toddlers in the development of autonomy
3. outline possible causes of anger outbursts (*temper tantrums*)
4. describe at least two ways to help toddlers cope with temper tantrums
5. describe use of reinforcement, modeling, and verbal disapproval in teaching toddlers the skills necessary to fit into their environment
6. outline suggestions for helping toddlers develop a positive self-concept
7. discuss ways to encourage development of a wide range of expectations in regard to sex roles

Interaction with Other Children

Exploring toddlers are interested in people, as well as in things. They appear to be attracted to other children, and seem to be just beginning to realize that children have a great deal in common, and that there is similarity between toddlers. They also seem to have begun to realize that there are even similarities between themselves and the new adults they encounter. Thus, the way all these individuals react to toddlers influences the way they feel about other people, and about themselves as unique, developing human beings.

According to Snyder, Piaget emphasizes interactions with peers as the principal means for overcoming children's egocentrism in learning.[1] For as much as they enjoy their own personal explorations and delight in adult participation, toddlers become increasingly interested in experiences with other children. Although most babies laugh at and enjoy watching or being entertained by older children, during toddlerhood a different type of relationship develops.

These children show interest in other toddlers as people and progress in their ability to play together. Let's review the development of play as it contributes to interaction among children.

Initially, infants and young toddlers play either alone or with adults. Then, gradually, toddlers become aware of each other for longer periods of time. We observed two toddlers (eighteen and twenty months old) becoming acquainted. They began by poking at each other's eyes (a common action) and progressed through hair, ears, mouths, hands, and clothes. The amount of staring and touching time was approximately four minutes and ended abruptly when the twenty-month-old pushed the other while trying to examine the eighteen-month-old's diaper pins (he himself was wearing training pants).

You have read, and perhaps observed, that toddlers progress from solitary to parallel, onlooker, and cooperative play, although throughout early childhood they may engage in any of these forms. During these play periods, confrontations between toddlers often arise as they begin to form relationships with each other. These conflicts may occur over ownership of toys and materials. Toddlers are extremely possessive of things that belong to them and of things temporarily in their possession. Many toddlers become very upset at finding another child in "my chair," or perhaps with "my doll," or reading "my book." One two-year-old, on seeing a crawling infant approach her ball, shouted, "John-John, me ball, no! You football! Stop!" And the same little girl teased an older toddler about possession of his mother. She pointed at his mother and announced, "Me mama." He replied, "No, she's my mama." She continued negatively shaking her head and insisting that his mother was actually her mother when indeed her own mother was present at the time.

Even when two toddlers play together with materials that belong to the center, conflicts arise over possession. They may become very upset if their neighbors borrow blocks, rings, or other toys that they have gotten out and therefore "own" by previous possession if not actual ownership.

No words from the teacher, or insistence that children share with their friends, can help the situation, and they may actually harm the children's relationship. Toddlers simply are not capable of sharing as adults define the word. Piaget has shown that toddlers do not have the ability to see something from other people's point of view.[2]

PLAY GUIDANCE TO MINIMIZE CONFLICT

Since toddlers cannot experience each other's feelings, you can expect many periods of conflicts, as all egocentric toddlers want to have their own way. You can attempt to minimize the conflicts by having a variety of materials to attract their interest.

By rotating your equipment and material, you can

provide possibilities for new experiences daily. Toddlers who are encouraged to explore will probably find many interesting things to do. Several toddlers may discover an exciting toy at the same time. If you find that several toddlers are interested in a hand mirror in the play house, it may be possible to purchase additional mirrors so several children can play at the same time.

Fortunately, toddlers are easily distracted and often can be interested in another toy or activity. When conflict arises between two toddlers, however, the adult in charge must protect the rights of the child who originally had possession of the toy, without lectures on the value of sharing. Perhaps a simple explanation would be appropriate—a statement that you cannot let the second child take the toy and that you would not allow someone to take things from him or her. Making children share is not in keeping with their abilities, and forced sharing is not actually sharing at all.

Teachers and parents who are anxious to have polite, sharing children sometimes use physical force to encourage toddlers' cooperation. The authors are strongly opposed to any form of slapping or spanking of children. We feel that it encourages negative behavior by providing a model for using force with other human beings.

In their research on modeling, Bandura and associates have set forth the importance of understanding that aggression depends on the amount of physical aggression displayed in a group.[3] Observing aggressive behavior seems to be sufficient to learn that behavior—there is evidence that children who see physical aggression more readily imitate it. It appears likely that children who are spanked do more hitting of other children than do children who have been talked with and redirected toward acceptable activities.

Toddlers' feelings must be considered. Physical punishment seems to contribute to feelings of conflict within toddlers. They are curious beings, who want to explore their environment and experiment with relationships with others. Their curiosity needs to be encouraged. They do not need to be burdened with the fear that, if they do not always behave as adults would like, they will be spanked or forced into compliance.

This is not to suggest that toddlers can completely control their own lives. Limits must be set, to protect them from their environment, from others, and from themselves. But these limits should permit and encourage learning, and adults who care for developing toddlers must respect areas of conflict. As toddlers learn about the people and things in their environment, they develop a better understanding of their capabilities and limitations. They gain self-confidence, increase their sense of autonomy, and form more realistic self-concepts.

Autonomy and Self-Control

As toddlers learn that they can do things for and by themselves, their concept of themselves alters. They are no longer helpless babies, but neither are they fully capable people. This situation creates a conflict over dependence and independence, as they struggle for balance in order to develop an accurate self-concept and a feeling of self-control. Toddlerhood is a critical period in children's development of a sense of autonomy, which may be defined as their desire and determination to be independent.

Observations seem to indicate that infants are not aware of their separateness from their environment. They have to discover that their hands are not just another toy, but a part of them that they can control and move at will. As they progress into toddlerhood, their awareness of being separate from their environment increases, and they begin to form concepts of what they are. There is so much they can do, yet so much they can't do.

They take one small step as infants and it turns into a

giant leap for autonomy in toddlerhood. With their first steps, infants become toddlers, working their way toward independence and greater autonomy. And probably shouting all the way, the one thing that seems to be the trademark of toddlers' demand for independence, "No, no, no!" Their wavering between positive independence and negative dependence is evident in their vocalizations. Often they say no when they mean yes or perhaps maybe. One toddler insisted that he did not want a cookie as his mother laid it on his plate. While he was saying no, he picked it up, ate it, and commented on how good it was. Alternately and simultaneously, toddlers need to be free and secure, independent and dependent.

ENCOURAGING AUTONOMY

Toddlers, in comparison with infants, have acquired many new motor skills and mental abilities. They are proud of their accomplishments. They want to do things by themselves, even things that they are not capable of doing. You can acknowledge their capabilities and try to cooperate with them in their activities. Toddlers should not be burdened with adult fears for their safety, because overprotectiveness frustrates and confuses them. They want to explore but they are aware of adult anxiety. This can create conflict between their need for security and their desire for freedom. Your degree of acceptance of their alternating feelings will be seen in the manner in which you attempt to aid toddlers.

Assistance. Adults must expect, and respect, abrupt changes in toddlers. Most of the time, toddlers will insist on a "do-it-myself" procedure and they should be permitted to try. If they decide they need help, they should not be teased or ignored. They should be helped by understanding adults. When children need, ask for, and receive help, they learn that the world is a friendly place where needs will be met. This gives them confidence to attempt other tasks, secure in the knowledge that they do not always have to succeed.

However, if adults do not allow toddlers to develop in independence and autonomy, they encourage negative feelings within the children. When they force assistance toddlers neither want nor ask for, they reduce the toddler's confidence in being allowed to try new experiences. The toddlers feel they cannot depend on others or on themselves. They feel they have no control over themselves or their environments.

One mother with a do-it-myself toddler insisted on putting shoes on her child, who insisted on doing it herself. The mother picked up the toddler and put the shoes on. The child went limp, then began to cry and kick repeatedly, screaming, "Me do it!" Finally, when the ordeal was over and she was sitting on the floor, the child jerked the shoes off and screamed, "Do it all by meself!" The mother, aware that she had been too forceful, apologized and offered to untie the shoes so that her daughter could try again to put them on by herself.

Occasionally a parent or teacher will find it necessary to rush toddlers or do something for them that they would like to do for themselves. Although this may anger the children, it need not shame them, unless it occurs too often. Events such as described above, repeated consistently, will have severe negative effects on children's ability to develop feelings of autonomy and self-control.

As children develop in these areas, greater conflict with adults may arise. Toddlers will want to do more by themselves and may resist and resent adult interference. More verbal toddlers may say that they want to do it themselves; the less verbal may scream, "No, no, no!" and react with physical aggression. Adults who expect this conflict will not take these behaviors as a personal insult, but will realize that they are part of the development of autonomy and self-control.

Consistent criticism, forcing, and shaming toddlers create in them a doubt as to their capabilities as people.

They lack enough autonomy to develop healthy personalities. On the other hand, children who constantly have their own way live in an unrealistic setting that cannot long endure: they have too much autonomy to develop healthy personalities. Children must learn that self-control sometimes may mean being able to do what they want to do. At other times, it may mean accepting not being able to do what they want. When toddlers are not allowed to have their way or do things themselves, they may become angry. This anger may be released in the form of a tantrum.

TEMPER TANTRUMS

Temper tantrums are one way in which children both display and release their anger and frustration. During tantrums children may throw themselves on the floor, kick, scream and pound with their hands, feet, and head. Or the tantrum may take the form of running, screaming, or hitting a toy, an animal, a table, chair, or another person. (And realistically, we must note that adults also participate in tantrums, but theirs are a bit more discreetly conducted, as in speeding in the car.)

An occasional tantrum is to be expected from toddlers. You must realize that it is a reaction to great frustration. Adults who remain calm and confident will reassure upset children, who are frightened by their own anger and aggression. Adults who show anger or embarrassment will only increase toddlers' frustration.

Coping with tantrums. There are no set rules on how to deal with a frustrated, angry toddler. Each child and each situation are unique and need individual response. However, the three most common ways of dealing with tantrums are to distract, ignore, and give in to or encourage the actions of toddlers.

Fortunately, toddlers are easily distracted. We observed a thirteen-month-old experiencing her first tantrum in a large shopping mall because her mother would not allow her to go into a certain store. The toddler threw herself on the sidewalk, kicking, and screaming. As people stared, the embarrassed mother picked her up and carried her off. As they walked, the mother tried to interest the toddler in other sights of the mall.

Some adults attempt to cope by ignoring the tantrum. We have observed this technique both succeed and fail. In one successful scene, the caregiver ignored the tantrum by walking to another part of the room. The toddler immediately got up from the floor, ran over in front of the adult, threw herself down, and began her act again. When the adult again turned out of visual range, the toddler got up, ran to the adult, and demanded, "Watch me crying!" at which time they both began laughing. That tantrum ended but another adult who ignored was not so fortunate; that child's tantrum continued for ten minutes before the adult took the child outdoors where he could run off his anger.

A third way to deal with tantrums is to give in to the child's demands. This, however, seems to encourage their recurrence. One toddler ate his popsicle and wanted a second. His caregiver refused his request. He threw a tantrum. The caregiver handed him another popsicle in order to stop his screaming. Of course, his tantrums are now frequent because they get the results he wants.

Avoiding tantrums. Temper tantrums that occur frequently (several times a day) may be caused by children's becoming overtired or being physically ill. Occasional tantrums are probably brought on by toddlers' environments, which may have too many restricting items and people. An outdoor environment, organized to allow toddlers to run, climb, push, pull, and move freely, without constant adult restrictions, will help reduce frustration and release children's energy. The same is true of an indoor environment arranged so that untouchable items are out of sight and reach of toddlers and provided with objects such as pounding benches or musical instruments for release of energy.

Some temper tantrums cannot be avoided. They are a common reaction from toddlers who are angry and frustrated and developing a sense of autonomy. However, by providing an environment that allows for release of physical energies and establishes a minimum of restraints on children, tantrums may be reduced to a minimum in the day care center.

BEHAVIOR MODIFICATION

Like the term "temper tantrum," the term "behavior modification" may produce negative feelings in adults. When we hear "temper tantrum," we often picture children trying to manipulate adults. (Billy wants a sucker. Mother refuses. Billy has a temper tantrum, thus hoping to alter her response.) When we hear "behavior modification" we may picture the adult trying to manipulate the child. (Mother wants Billy to pick up his toys. Billy refuses. Mother offers Billy a sucker if he picks up his toys, thus hoping to alter his response.)

Behavior modification does provide the adult with considerable power to change children's behavior. This power must be handled very carefully. Reinforcing positive behavior and ignoring, when possible, negative behavior is an acceptable method of behavior modification. Punishment, for example, the practice of isolation through "time out," is not an acceptable method for use with toddlers. It may give toddlers bad feelings about themselves and hinder their development of a positive self-concept.

Self-Concept

Observing toddlers' everyday behavior may help you gain insight into their feelings about themselves. The self-concept, which we defined as how people see themselves, and *self-esteem*, which is the value they place on themselves, originate from four main sources: other people's comments; the toddlers' own experiences; their ability to live up to expectations and goals set for and by themselves; and their own ability to evaluate themselves.[4]

Development of self-concept is, as it sounds, a very complex process. It is also a very important part of life and in toddlerhood is closely related to the development of autonomy. As toddlers begin to see themselves as separate, independent, capable people, they begin to develop positive self-concepts. As their caregiver, you can help them in this development.

Toddlers are anxious to please the adults who are close to them. They will attempt new activities, repeat words, or resist doing things they would like to do in order to receive your approval. You can advance their development of a positive self-image by encouraging them in new adventures and praising them for success. When you minimize their possibilities for failures you help eliminate negative feelings about their inability to accomplish tasks.

One way to contribute to a positive self-concept is to help toddlers feel that you care about them as people and that you can accept their positive and negative feelings. Another way is to reassure them that they are important to you even when they have tantrums, spill their milk, break toys, lose puzzle pieces, or wet their pants. And although toddlers do not seem to be aware of ethnic or economic differences in each other, many are aware of their own sexuality. Helping children understand that you accept each as male or female and that you are pleased with their particular sex is another way to encourage a positive self-concept.

SEX-ROLE CONCEPT

One's total self-concept is influenced by his *sex-role concept*. Considering the changing sex roles of our society, there is bound to be some confusion as to appropriate sex roles for children. First, we must consider the typical sex-related behavior of the toddlers and how their environment has influenced this behavior, in order to understand how to encourage appropriate behavior.

Toddlers' behavior. Among adults there seems to be some confusion as to what is appropriate *sex-typed* behavior for children from twelve to thirty months old. However, among the toddlers, no confusion and no concern is apparent. One observation study of toddlers noted that very little sex-typed behavior is exhibited during toddlerhood, although such behavior occurrences do increase with age.[5] These children seem to participate in a variety of activities without regard to the appropriateness of their sexes.

Perhaps this combined behavior is a result of not being aware of prescribed sexual roles. Also, the modeling process certainly must be a contributing factor. Traditionally, young children have been cared for in the home by the mother. If the mother worked, they were cared for in homes, nurseries, or day care centers, staffed by women. Because the children's sleeping schedules and the parents' working schedules differed, infants and toddlers often spent relatively short periods of their days with a father figure. Therefore, their modeling behavior has involved typical household chores conducted by the mother or caregiver. We therefore find toddling boys and girls, dressed in high-heeled shoes, aprons, and hats, feeding the baby, sweeping the floor, washing dishes, and folding the laundry. However, both sexes also engaged in what are often labeled male activities, such as carrying out trash, washing the car, painting the wall, and digging in the garden. Thus we find a coordination of all types of activities familiar to the daily routine of toddlers. During toddlerhood, there is almost complete absence of statements like, "Boys don't do that," and other sex-typed behavior.

Materials to encourage activities. As toddlers engage in their creative activities, their environment affects their play. You can help to provide a suitable environment by furnishing a variety of play materials. As we have mentioned, dolls, along with their clothes and furniture, are welcome props that encourage role playing. Dress-up clothes should represent all kinds of employment, such as a mailman's hat and a fluffy apron, to encourage playing out so-called male and female roles. Once props are provided, the toddlers can use them creatively. If a boy wants to wear the apron and cook supper, that is acceptable, just as the girl wearing the mail carrier's hat, delivering the letter, is acceptable. Toddlers should be encouraged to act out feelings and interests without regard to stereotyped sex roles.

Encouraging sex-role concept.   Although there is some confusion as to appropriate sex-typed behavior for children, it is perfectly clear that adults' opinions and attitudes affect toddlers' self-concepts, including their feelings of sexuality.

Dictating "appropriate" sex roles begins early in children's lives. Note the typical birth gifts of a miniature football for a son, as compared to a soft, pink, fuzzy ball for a daughter. And at age two, the little boy receives a train, while the little girl receives a doll. Little boys need play experiences with dolls and softness just as much as little girls need play experiences with movement and solid objects. We have seen that, if left to themselves, they will experiment freely with all materials. Unfortunately, many adults are too concerned with establishing stereotyped sex-roles in young children.

Following the observation study of toddlers mentioned earlier, the toddlers' mothers were interviewed. They stressed the traditional sex-typed behavior and provided sex-typed toys for their toddlers. They wanted their boys to be able to fight back and not to cry. They wanted their girls to be sweet, dainty, and helpless. It is interesting to note, however, that the maternal attitudes had no observable effect on the toddlers' behavior.

The authors feel strongly that adults who care for young children must avoid stiffling feelings and putting

children into narrow molds. Caregivers and parents together need to realize the importance of letting toddlers express their feelings. This means that girls and boys both can cry, be sensitive, and show gentleness. Both can be competitive, ambitious, and physically strong.

An adult who tries to guide toddlers into a society whose sex roles are in the midst of change must be particularly sensitive to their future needs. You can aid children's appreciation and understanding of maleness and femaleness by helping them in the correct use of the words boy and girl, he and she. (Toddlers often use the terms interchangeably.) Also, you can encourage each child to accept his or her gender, stressing the fact that you accept and like the sex of each child. Avoid any inference of male or female superiority. Through your acceptance, you can reinforce children without limiting opportunities or possibilities for either sex.

During toddlerhood, when sex-typed behavior is not a concern for the children, you have the opportunity to reinforce human sexuality, a positive self-concept, and the worth of each person as a unique individual, regardless of color, ethnic background, or sexual identity.

Challenge to the Caregiver

Caring for toddlers is indeed a demanding job. Many major goals are accomplished during this period between twelve and thirty months of age. As the caregiver, you must be constantly alert in order to keep these independent, dependent, walking babies from physical harm, caused by lack of judgment, and mental or emotional harm, caused by lack of consideration. They have the desire but not the ability to challenge the entire environment of people and things. You must be protective, but not overly protective. You must be encouraging and supportive, but within limits. Your attitude is a vital influence on the present and future development of the toddlers, so you must exercise every precaution in your attempt to meet their needs.

ANTICIPATING TODDLERS' NEEDS

During the first months of toddlerhood, children discover that they can move about on their own and that there is a world of new experiences awaiting them. They attempt to experiment with, explore, look at, touch, and taste everything they come in contact with. They try to shake, squeeze, rattle, pull out, and get into everything; all at one time. They are determined to climb on top of, underneath, and into anything, large or small. Doors that they never opened, drawers that they never pulled, shelves that they never explored are all of utmost importance now. They are exploring and learning and do not plan to miss anything.

Toddlers *must* explore. They learn by exploring. Through your interest and concern in their exploring for physical development, you advance their development in language and thought and help them to learn self-awareness and self-control. They depend on you for support and encouragement in all types of explorations.

ENCOURAGING TODDLERS

Enjoy their explorations. Encourage them when they attempt new activities, such as making the train move by pushing with their own feet rather than sitting on it, crying to be pulled. Praise them when they climb into the large cardboard box and crawl out through one of the holes. Appreciate their new-found ability to ring the bell or shake the sound cylinder. Laugh with them when they enjoy the surprise of the pop-up characters in the vinyl books. Be enthusiastic when they attempt to climb

on and off of the riding horse, up and down the stairs, into and out of chairs. Show pleasure when they build a tower with blocks, throw balls, pull toys, follow directions, identify objects, turn pages, drink from straws, open boxes, turn on light switches, snap beads together, stack rings, or unscrew lids. Enjoy their humor when they put baskets on their heads, turn around in circles, dance to music, walk like monsters, play hide and seek, or giggle at being chased. Show your approval when they combine words, sing songs, repeat rhymes, label colors, identify pictures, make marks on paper, talk to themselves, share with friends, play cooperatively, eat dinners, wet in the potty, put on their sweaters, pick up their toys, pedal tricycles, put their scraps in the wastebasket, or learn new words. Accept them as people when in frustration they lash out at people or things, cry because they are sad, pout because they are excluded, quit because they are mad, grab because they are hungry, bite because they are afraid, hit because they are hurt, scream because they are forced, or spit because their feelings have been stepped on. Comfort them when they have poor self-concepts. Be exuberant with them when their whole being cries out, "I'm me and it's great to be me!"

In that period of eighteen months, there is so much joy to discover, so much growing to do, so much socialization to acquire. As the caregiver, you are needed. Be there. And as toddlerhood ends you will know that your presence was significant in encouraging their progression from toddlers to preschool children.

Glossary

Self-concept Individual's awareness of how he or she is like and different from others.

Self-esteem The value the individual places on himself or herself.

Sex-role concept   One's ideas concerning the behavior that is appropriate for each sex.

Sex-typed   Behavior and toys traditionally associated with either males or females.

Temper tantrum   Display and release of anger and frustration. Often children will roll on the floor, kicking, screaming, and banging their arms or heads.

Study Questions

1. Discuss the importance of the development of autonomy.
2. Describe ways in which an adult can encourage and discourage toddlers' development of autonomy.
3. Observe a toddler experiencing a tantrum. What brought it on? How did the adult cope with it?
4. Discuss ways in which children and adults influence the development of self-concept.
5. Invite a day care director or teacher to discuss with your class the sex-role concept in toddlers. Include in your discussion how parents and teachers affect children's sex-type behavior.

Notes

1. M. Snyder, "The Developing Self: Nurturance in School," in *The Child and His Image*, ed. K. Yamamoto, Houghton Mifflin, Boston, 1972, p. 70.
2. D. Elkind, "Giant in the Nursery School—Jean Piaget," in *Annual Editions Readings in Human Development '73–'74*, Dushkin Publishing Group, Guilford, Connecticut, 1973, p. 4.
3. A. Bandura, D. Ross, and S. A. Ross, "Transmission of Aggression Through Imitation of Aggressive

Models," *Journal of Abnormal Social Psychology*, 63, 1961, p. 580.

4. S. Coopersmith, *The Antecedents of Self-Esteem*, W. W. Freeman, San Francisco, 1967.

5. N. Busch, "Gender Identity in Toddlerhood," *Merrill-Palmer Newsletter*, 14, no. 4, 1973.

Supplementary Readings

Baker, K. R., and X. Fane. *Understanding and Guiding Young Children*. Prentice-Hall, Englewood Cliffs, 1971.

Brazelton, T. B. "How To Set Limits for Toddlers." *Redbook*, August, 1973.

Lewis, M. "Culture and Gender Roles: There's No Unisex in the Nursery." *Psychology Today*, May, 1972.

Richardson, F. *For Parents Only*. McKay, New York, 1962.

Spock, B. "Helping Children To Express Anger." *Redbook*, April, 1973.

———. "When Your Toddler Is Afraid to Let You Go." *Redbook*, September, 1973.

Wolfe, K. *As Your Child Grows*. Child Study Association of America, New York, 1955.

5

The Preschool Child's Body, Language, and Thought

After reading this chapter you should be able to:

1. describe changes in size and shape of the body during the preschool years
2. outline ways you can influence nutrition and health of preschool children
3. outline suggestions for helping preschool children develop gross motor skills and ability to coordinate the small muscles of hand and wrist
4. discuss influences on language development of preschool children
5. discuss helping children with *information gaining and processing*
6. discuss developing *creativity* in preschool children
7. discuss relationship between skills learned during preschool years and skills in reading, writing, and arithmetic developed during the school years
8. discuss limitations of the *IQ test* in evaluating preschool children's thinking ability

The landmarks in children's development result from a combination of forces—their inherited developmental time schedules and their past and present experiences in home and in day care. We stated earlier that these landmarks must be taken as. general expectations. You must be even more cautious with the landmarks given in this chapter.

The development of preschool children varies even more widely than that of infants and toddlers. There are many reasons for this greater variation, and the most obvious one is the longer period of time during which the environment has influenced the children. This chapter's landmarks should help you focus your attention as you observe and determine the skills of children in your care. Fitting your expectations and the learning experiences you provide to each child's abilities is essential for the children's best development and your own satisfaction. Consider the frustration for both adult and children when the adult planned a creative activity involving tying knots for three-year-old children who found this skill impossible for them.

Landmarks for Growth of the Body

Changes in height and weight during the preschool period are less dramatic than during infancy and toddlerhood. Between ages three and five, the average gain in weight is ten pounds and for height, around six inches. Change in body shape is more obvious than change in size. Chubby toddlers with protruding abdomens and short legs change to slender six-year-olds. Legs grow more rapidly during these years, as compared with the growth rate of the upper part of the body. A large part of the weight increase is due to the growth of the muscles. Consequently you can expect older preschool children to show more strength and endurance.

Preschool children are becoming increasingly responsible for selecting what they will eat. Children of this age have had plenty of time to develop specific likes and dislikes in foods, for example, to have become "hooked" on sweets. Preschoolers are often less active than toddlers. This lower activity level, coupled with a relatively slow rate of growth, may cause children to be "picky eaters." Since nutrition is a very important factor in children's strength, weight, resistance to disease, and energy level, the nutrition education they receive in day care is important during the preschool years as well as throughout life.

You may not be able to plan or even influence the menus in the center, but you can influence the children's acceptance of a variety of foods. Most important is the example you set in eating the foods with them. Through your interest in the children's eating, you can help them modify eating behavior if this seems desirable.

It has been generally thought that children can be expected to eat what they require for a balanced diet. This is a misconception based on a study that showed that newly weaned infants could select a balanced diet from a limited number of raw or cooked cereals, eggs, fruits, and vegetables.[1] No sugar or any type of dessert was included. These infants lived in a hospital setting where they had no opportunity to eat foods other than those selected by the researcher. It is important to note that they had no opportunity to acquire the taste for sweets that seems to make plain fruits and vegetables uninteresting for children.

Guiding children's eating requires your interest without overconcern. Some centers require children to taste all foods or to eat a specific amount of certain foods before they are permitted dessert. Children can be encouraged to taste new or disliked foods without always being forced to eat a food. Forcing food or praising children for "clean plates" seems questionable when many children and adults are overweight. You can limit the number of servings of liked foods, such as milk and bread, so that all the children at your table have more appetite for tasting the new food. Perhaps the single most important influence is the adult's praise for trying a new food or a previously disliked food.

Setting standards for table manners too high also may influence children's attitude toward eating. Children learn table manners through copying the behavior of the adults who eat with them. Preschool children are not as messy eaters as the toddlers, but they still need both hands and eating utensils to get food to their mouths.

Learning about food also encourages eating. Preschool children are ready to learn about chickens and cows, how seeds sprout, and where apples grow. Growing vegetables, along with the many cooking experiences that are possible in most centers, encourages children to explore new tastes as well as provides opportunity to learn a number of different concepts.

Sometimes day care workers become so involved in the mechanics of the mealtime routine that they miss an opportunity to use this period of the day as a learning experience for children. Sitting at a table with an adult, children gain experience in carrying on a conversation and comparing their ideas with those of others. The listening adult can learn of children's interests or obvious gaps in information that provide ideas for ongoing curriculum planning.

HEALTH

Children's health has a marked influence on their behavior. Preschool children have more resistance to disease than younger children, but many preschool children have frequent colds and other upper respiratory infections.

Day care centers vary, but an increasing number of centers permit children with colds to participate in center activities. Children with colds or other minor infections can cope with fewer demands, need more rest, and want less food than usual. Sometimes these children need help to go at a slower pace. Preschool children can learn health rules like covering nose and mouth with a Kleenex when they sneeze. Although adults in day care may be less anxious about children's minor illnesses than earlier in this century, they should continue to be aware of the importance of health for best development.

FATIGUE

Fatigue influences food consumption and children's ability to make the best use of experiences offered in the program. Fatigue also influences the behavior of both staff and children. Adults and children must learn to pace themselves to cope with the long day in a group of people of varying maturity levels. Sensitive, easily overstimulated children may find day care difficult unless they have interested adults to help them relax and get the rest they need.

Planned naptime after lunch ignores the varying needs of individual children. Having a room where children can rest whenever they are tired is ideal. Unfortunately, most centers must use the same space for play activities, eating, and resting. In these situations, a group naptime is necessary, but not all the children have to rest in the same way. Sleeping is not essential for resting.

Some children, particularly five-year-olds, can relax by looking at books or working puzzles, but they would be miserable tossing and turning on a cot in a darkened room. All children should not be expected to remain on cots for the same length of time. No children should be expected to remain on cots for more than half an hour to an hour if they cannot fall asleep. Children who sleep should be permitted to get up as soon as they awaken. Since children are more likely to have toilet accidents when they are half awake at the end of a nap, getting the children up when they awaken reduces the number of wet cots. Early risers after a nap have an opportunity for conversation with an adult alone—an experience all too often missing in group day care.

Landmarks in Control of the Body

GROSS MOTOR SKILLS

Health and nutrition together with changing body contour and growth of muscle tissue affect children's use of their bodies during this period. As the legs become longer in relation to total body length, children are better able to hop on one foot, skip, and run with ease. Following the cephalocaudal trend in development (defined in Chapter 1), skills in coordinating the legs are still emerging. The increase in muscle tissue contributes to children's strength and endurance.

INFLUENCE OF PLAYGROUND, EQUIPMENT, AND GUIDANCE

Environment has an even greater influence on the emergence of skills that are an elaboration of walking, like hopping and skipping, than on the walking itself. Helping children develop and practice emerging motor skills is just as important as helping them develop competence in thinking. When so many people are observers rather than participants in sports, children need to develop skills that can serve as a basis for satisfying sports experiences as they grow older. Skills in climbing, running, and tricycle-riding help children develop the feeling of being capable people—in other words, a positive self-concept.

Workers in day care may not be able to change a barren playground, but they can influence the outdoor activities part of the program through their interest in children's large-muscle activities, suggestions for purchase of small pieces of equipment, arrangement of existing equipment, and guidance. In selecting equipment for gross motor activities, give some thought to opportunities for these activities outside the center. Children who have tricycles and a place to ride them at home have less need for tricycles at the day care center than children who have never seen a tricycle.

Climbing experiences at home are most frequently lacking in many parts of the country. Most centers have some type of jungle gym for climbing, and adults can make the most of it through arrangement of supplementary equipment, approval for climbing, and enforcement of safety rules to minimize children's fear of climbing. A few cleated planks placed on sawhorses around a jungle gym in different patterns will attract children who already have mastered climbing the jungle gym and forgotten about it. Walking across a board a few feet from the ground is an introduction to climbing for children who are afraid to try the jungle gym itself. Few centers can afford to give space to any stationary climbing equipment indoors, but sawhorses and planks can be moved indoors on rainy days.

Adult interest, approval, and suggestions for activities can make the difference between random running around a barren playground and constructive large-muscle activities. Unfortunately, as a result of experience in the public schools, some adults think of outdoor play as a time when children can be left on their own as long as they do not hurt each other, while adults visit with each other. Many children will practice climbing, running, and jumping without encouragement from an adult, but less skillful and timid children often need adult encouragement to use these opportunities for developing large motor skills. Adult presence near a piece of equipment often encourages its use. Praise when children have just learned a skill encourages them to work to improve, and to work on other skills. Sometimes adults need to supply ideas for activities. Running with children on a cold day and devising simple games like dodge-ball bring new interest to outdoor activities. In games, preschool children usually see little need for rules and frequently change them. Whatever ground rules satisfy the children should be acceptable to the adults.

Helping children learn safety rules to avoid accidents is important during these years. Even minor accidents can be frightening to the children involved, as well as to others who see them. Rules will vary according to the playground and the children. Some rules that should be enforced on most playgrounds are holding tight with both hands while climbing, never pushing in high places, and riding tricycles without bumping into each other.

FINE MOTOR SKILLS

There are even fewer specific landmarks in development of finger and wrist control, or fine motor skills, than for gross motor skills at this period. Research in fine motor skills has involved such tasks as ability to copy a circle, square, or cross, or tie children's own shoes. Copying a circle or a cross also involves being able to see the shape, place that shape, and understand how to make one like it. You will note in Table 3 that three- to four-year-old children may be expected to copy a circle and a cross. At the four- to six-year-old period, they may learn to copy a square and a triangle. The research on which this knowledge is based is valuable in pointing up the sequence for learning these skills, but age level is tentative, because so much depends on the children's interest and experience with pencil and paper.

You will be quite aware of the children's lack of skill in use of their hands and fingers. Many adults are surprised that most children cannot tie their shoes until age five or perhaps later. The amount of food spilled at the lunch table is evidence of the difficulty of handling spoon or fork. Preschool children only gradually become independent in dressing as they learn buttoning, zipping, and tying.

Adults at home and in the center frequently overestimate children's ability to use their hands. They seem to value children's ability to print their names, draw recognizable pictures, and handle scissors easily more than their ability to run, climb, and skip. Yet, most children are awkward in printing, drawing, and cutting with scissors even toward the end of this period.

Guiding children in activities requiring fine motor skills requires giving freedom to select from a range of

TABLE 3 *Landmarks of Development*

PHYSICAL, MOTOR, AND LANGUAGE DEVELOPMENT	SOCIAL DEVELOPMENT
2½–3 years	
Runs smoothly	Grows possessive about toys
Uses short sentences	Enjoys playing alongside another child
Size at 3 years: 32–33 pounds, 37–38 inches	Gives orders
	Insists on rigid sameness of routine
3–4 years	
Stands on one leg, draws a circle and a cross (4 years)	Displays intense curiosity, asks questions
Completes sentences of 6–8 words (4 years)	Plays cooperatively with other children
Has become self-sufficient in many routines of home life	Shows interest in other children's bodies (3–5 years)
Size at 4 years: 38–40 pounds, 40–41 inches	
4–6 years	
Skips, broad jumps, dresses self	Generally prefers play with other children
Copies a square and a triangle (5 years)	Becomes competitive
Talks clearly, has mastered basic grammar, relates a story	Shows evidence of responsibility and guilt
Size at 5 years: 42–43 pounds, 43–44 inches	

SOURCE: Adapted from Boyd R. McCandless and Ellis Evans, *Children and Youth: Psychosocial Development,* Dryden Press, Hinsdale, Illinois, 1973, pp. 13–14, and Charles P. Smith, *Child Development,* William C. Brown, New York, 1966, pp. 8–9. Reprinted by permission of Dryden Press and Charles P. Smith.

materials that have one correct way of being used, like puzzles. For art activities, children should have large crayons, large paint brushes, large sheets of paper, and freedom to develop techniques in using them. In an effort to impress parents with what the child is doing in the program, some centers push children into demanding, uncreative projects like cutting out hearts following a line the teacher has drawn, or coloring within the lines in coloring books. In addition to discouraging creativity, these activities are too demanding for preschool children. A good general plan for guidance is to use a variety of materials that require coordination of the fingers, with freedom to leave the activity when tired. Recognition of the children's hard work and developing skill is important in this, as in other areas of behavior.

Landmarks in Language Development

Most children experience a kind of language explosion during toddlerhood and into preschool years.[2] In addition to rapid vocabulary growth, preschool children use increasingly complex sentences more effectively for a variety of purposes.

VOCABULARY

There are marked individual differences in vocabulary at any age. According to one study, vocabulary increases from around 450 words at thirty months to over 2500 words at age six.[3] There are fewer errors in pronunciation, but there are still sounds that are frequently mispronounced, as "wabbit" for "rabbit." The child's speech changes from one in which nouns predominate to speech that is similar to the adult norm.

GRAMMAR

Another obvious change during this period is the emergence of lengthier, more complex sentences. Children apparently depend less on the environment in learning grammar than in learning vocabulary, though you remember that speech sounds in babbling in infancy seem to evolve from a built-in capacity to produce a variety of sounds. *Psycholinguists* (scientists who study the relationship of language to characteristics of the language-user) have provided some interesting theories as to how children learn rules of grammar, but there is not one generally accepted theory.

It is clear that training procedures have relatively little influence on grammatical knowledge and that children are remarkably uniform in the sequence, though not the age level, of mastering of certain forms of grammar, like "in" and "on."[4] Apparently the environment provides the information from which children develop a set of rules, as can be noted in their use of words like "goed," "digged," and "sheeps."[5] Correcting grammar has little influence on children, as shown by the following exchange:

NEIL: "I throwed the ball."
ADULT: "You threw it far. What did you do with the ball?"
NEIL: "I throwed it down the hill."
ADULT: "You mean you threw it."
NEIL: "Uh huh, I throwed it."

INFLUENCES ON LANGUAGE DEVELOPMENT

Direct teaching methods seem to have little influence on grammar, but adults influence other aspects of language development, especially vocabulary. One study showed that an important indicator of a child's vocabulary at a given age was the mother's test score on an adult vocabulary test.[6] As indicated in the chapters on infancy and toddlerhood, reinforcement of language through the adult's response is important in vocabulary development and use of language.

Communication style. Adults' *communication style* probably affects the way children learn to use language. Berenstein in England[7] and Hess and Shipman in their research with mothers and preschool children in Chicago have pointed out differences in the way mothers communicate and teach their children. The following example from the Hess and Shipman research point out these differences.[8]

1a. "I've got another game to teach you."

1b. "There's another thing you have to learn here, so sit down and pay attention."

2a. "Now listen to Mommy carefully and watch what I do because I'm going to show you how we play the game."

2b. "Pay attention now and get it right, 'cause you're gonna have to show the lady how to do it later."

3a. "No, Johnny. That's a big one. Remember, we're going to keep the big ones separate from the little ones."

3b. "No, that's not what I showed you! Put that with the big ones where it belongs."

4a. "Wait a minute, Johnny. You have to look at the block first before you try to find where it goes. Now pick it up again and look at it—is it big or small? . . . Now put it where it goes."

4b. "That doesn't go there—you're just guessing. I'm trying to show you how to do this and you're just putting them any old place. Now pick it up and do it again and this time don't mess up."

5a. "No, we can't stop now, Johnny. Mrs. Smith wants me to show you how to do this so you can do it for her. Now if you pay close attention and let Mommy teach you, you can learn how to do it and show her, and then you'll have some time to play."

5b. "Now you're playing around and you don't even know how to do this. You want me to call the lady? You better listen to what I'm saying and quit playing around or I'm gonna call the lady in on you and see how you like that."

If these data collected in a controlled situation described the day-to-day interaction of these mothers with their children, mother "a." provides greater variety of sentence structure along with giving reasons for her directions. Obviously one would expect child "a." to use more variety in his own speech and to gain more information to cope with similar problems in the future.

Acceptance of children's language style. The extent of imitation of communication style is not clear, but we are made suddenly aware of it when children imitate a word that is offensive to adults. Younger preschool children may repeat these words and forget about them when they are ignored. Older preschoolers are increasingly aware of the power of language, and even pick up nonverbal clues in the adult's reaction to specific words. Many preschool groups go through a period of "bathroom talk." Here is an example in a verse of a song sung to the tune of "London Bridge" in a nursery school:

> We do pee-pee on everybody
> on everybody
> on everybody
> We do pee-pee on everybody
> especially Dr. Highberger.

Many parents and staff in day care centers are shocked by bathroom talk and swearing from young children, but they accept swearing and "four-letter" words from adults. Possibly we overreact because we were punished for using this same type of language as children. How much of this language is accepted in a day care center should be a joint decision of staff and parents.

It seems to the authors that punishment for certain words at this time in development in learning to use language effectively as a means of self-expression may hinder the child's growth in spontaneous use of language. At the same time, these children can learn that most adults do not appreciate extensive use of bathroom terms at the lunch table. Giving freedom to experiment at certain times during the day could contribute to more creative use of language. In most preschool groups, bathroom talk is considered childish by children who are near the end of this age period.

Use of dialects also produces varying reactions in adults. Many people have the misconception that Standard English is a superior language to Black English or other dialects. Linguistic study of Black English shows that it is just as sophisticated a language as Standard English. Understanding and being able to communicate with children, using their own dialect, not only facilitates communication but also influences children's feelings about themselves and their families, who taught them the dialects they use. Your center may teach Standard English as a second language, since this is the language used by most people in this country, and it is the language children will encounter in the public schools. You should try to make children feel that their dialect is just as good a language, but a different language, when you are teaching Standard English.

FLUENCY

Repetition of a word's first sound or of an entire word may appear during this period. This is part of speech development for some children. It may be that the children are thinking faster than they can formulate the words. According to one authority who spent his life studying stuttering, stutterers are made through labeling this sound or word repetition as stuttering and making children aware of the label.[9] This may not be the only cause of stuttering but it is one in which the adult can make a difference.

Adults can also help by making children feel that the adults will listen as long as necessary for communication of their ideas. Since speech is a good barometer of the emotions, children may exhibit more repetition when under excessive pressure. Locating and alleviating the source of pressure on the children could help. Avoid asking them to repeat the words that have given them difficulty.

Ability to pronounce sounds correctly, or *articulation,* changes during this period. According to one study, the average ability of the three-year-old children examined was correct pronunciation of 63 percent of the sounds attempted as compared to 89 percent correctly pronounced sounds at age six.[10] Pronunciation skill varies, however. Some children's articulation improves more rapidly than others, probably for a variety of reasons.

A question often arises as to when to refer children who cannot be understood readily to a speech specialist. Children may outgrow the infantile speech, and being introduced to formal speech training too early in life may make them speech conscious and result in refusal to talk.[11] Informal practice of speech in conversations may solve the problem for many children. In advising parents on the matter of seeking help from a speech clinic, you should consider the age of the children, whether they can make themselves understood by adults and other children in spite of poor articulation, and possible causes for the apparent problem. If children are holding onto infantile speech in order to compete with a baby brother for attention, for example, speech training would work on the symptom, not the problem.

USE OF LANGUAGE

Most children develop language with little difficulty and language growth is accompanied by the ability to put language to a greater variety of uses. Collection of information through questions and improved memory through increased vocabulary (verbal symbols for storing information) are obvious. Less obvious, perhaps, is the ability to use language in controlling behavior. Controlling or attempting to control other children's behavior can be noted in verbalizations such as "You're s'posed to share" and "Don't throw sand," in groups of four- to six-year-olds. There is also evidence that language helps these children control their own behavior. According to a series of Russian experiments, two-and-one-half- and three-year-olds were able to repeat rules but were not able to use these rules to inhibit an action like squeezing a rubber bulb in an experimental situation.[12] But four-and-one-half- and five-and-one-half-year-olds could do this.

This research may explain why younger preschoolers have difficulty following obvious rules on sharing equipment and keeping the sand in the sandbox. It also points up the importance of continued verbalization of rules and the reasons behind them. Older preschool children are able to set up their own rules, with help from adults.

Landmarks in Development of Thinking Ability

Language facilitates the development of thinking. Through listening to children's speech, adults can learn about their thinking ability and gaps in their understanding. Children's development of thinking ability will be discussed in three sections: gaining information, processing information, and creativity in thinking. The educational tools, reading, writing, and arithmetic, are discussed in relation to skills being developed at the preschool-age level.

GAINING INFORMATION

Like infants and toddlers, preschool children are reaching for new information. But unlike the younger children, preschoolers can talk at length with an adult on a variety of topics. This verbal ability may encourage you to tell children the answer instead of giving them the chance to learn for themselves through observation.

The day care center helps children add to their background of information through a variety of planned experiences. This fund of information grows more rapidly, with fewer bits of misinformation, through first-hand experiences. Talking about a picture of a duck may help the child understand a little about ducks but is a poor substitute for a live duck that can be touched, listened to, and smelled as well as seen.

First-hand experiences, however, will bring about changes in the children's thought structures only if assimilation and accommodation take place, as described in Chapter 1. Everyone learns more efficiently if interested in the subject. Unfortunately, this fact is not often applied to group learning experiences because it is difficult to plan for the interests of all the individuals in a group. One controversial question in early childhood education is how much adult goals and how much the interest of each individual child should influence the curriculum. The authors' point of view is that both should be considered.

Some children are so eager for new information and new experiences that they readily respond to any visitor or field trip. Interest can be aroused in some children through pictures placed around the playroom at their eye level, discussion of the pictures, and questions. Other children are not ready for such experience and should be permitted to do something else. Responsible adults need to know which children are the nonparticipants and whether they are the same children month after month. Adults who think that all children in a group should go on every field trip are probably wasting somebody's time.

The most carefully planned experiences will not enable children to see the environment as adults see it. There is evidence for this in the conservation experiment described in Chapter 1. By age six, a few children become capable of conservation, though this ability usually comes around age seven. Children then can understand that it is possible to change the shape of a ball of clay without changing the quantity. As in developing rules of grammar, the ability to conserve cannot be taught directly; the children evolve this ability themselves, through a variety of experiences.

Direct experience does not provide all the information children need and want. Adults, other children, and books become increasingly important as sources of information. Preschool children ask many and often difficult questions to add to their store of information. Adults encourage independence in seeking information when they respond to questions by asking questions in return to help children think through the answers or help children find the answers in books. At times, adults can provide answers through a specially planned experience such as a trip to the farm in answer to the question "Where does milk come from?"

Questions such as "Where do babies come from?" and "Is that dead bird in heaven?" place considerable responsibility on the adult. These, like other questions, should be answered, but with an awareness of parental beliefs and what children are learning outside the center. Information as to where babies come from is factual knowledge and should be given to children. But children of this age are not ready for a lecture on the process of reproduction. How much information you give depends on the children's families and how much they seem to want to know. "The babies grow in their mothers' bodies," is generally a good beginning to questions about reproduction. Questions about death are different, because they involve religious beliefs, and parents are responsible for determining what their children are taught about religion. Preschool children all can learn that no one really knows what happens after death, and that people have a variety of different beliefs.

Trying to answer all children's questions, or looking up answers with the children, or promising to find answers are important in encouraging children to use questions for gaining information. Admitting to a mistaken answer when you have made one is also important

to maintain children's confidence in adults as sources of information.

PROCESSING INFORMATION

Preschoolers are more efficient than toddlers in processing information. This results from their increased ability to focus attention on one activity for a long period of time, to remember past experiences, and to manipulate language in thinking. Preschoolers are also more able to focus on what is important to them. In observing a visiting rabbit, they are able to note similarities and differences to other animals they have seen. If they have seen a cat but not a rabbit, they can note the similar fur and whiskers and the different ears and tail.

At this age, ability to focus attention on one activity is growing, but length of time spent on one activity still varies widely among children. As compared with older children and adults, most preschool children are unable to talk about one topic or remain with one activity for long. Adults are tempted to force children to sit still in a group to listen to a discussion. Comments such as "My daddy got a new car" when a group is discussing the visiting rabbit provide evidence that sitting still with the group may not show that children are paying attention to the discussion. These children may be learning to ignore what is going on around them, and, as a result, they may miss opportunities to learn. By observing closely you will know when children are giving attention to an activity and you can stop the activity when they begin to lose interest. Some children who have difficulty staying with a project to completion, like finishing a puzzle, can stay with it if an adult sits with them and possibly offers a helpful suggestion.

Classification (putting information into categories) is important in processing information. Preschool children are able to classify objects and events only according to one dimension. They may agree that the ball is a toy and a doll is a toy, but when asked whether there would be any toys left if all the balls were burned, they will probably say "no."

Based on an understanding of how children learn to process information, programs for preschool children use thinking games and stories. These games and stories involve activities like noting sequence of events (as in getting out of bed and getting dressed in the morning), noting likenesses and differences, and grouping objects that are alike or used together. Classification activities can be specifically planned, as in thinking games that require putting all the things that move in a group. Adults can help children in other activities, such as noting the similarities and differences in raw and cooked vegetables, or noting that the visiting rabbit and a cat are both animals.

These games are more successful in a situation where rules are flexible, children come and go according to interest, and there are no winners or losers. Preschool children like to win but they are poor losers. Specific rules and experience of losing are more appropriate for the school-age level. If these games are arranged for small groups, children do not have to wait a long time for a turn.

A wide variety of activities that emphasize classification are available from companies that produce materials for young children. You can develop your own from materials available in most centers. Some suggestions are given at the end of the chapter.

Some classification activities use circles, squares, and triangles of different sizes and colors. When using these materials, grouping according to size, color, or shape is more important than automatically giving the label "large red triangle." Learning the labels that fit with colors and shapes is a relatively simple memory activity. Children must be able to group materials to categorize according to which shapes and which colors are alike or different and to develop a categorization plan.

Thinking games also give children experience in developing several different possible solutions to a problem, often called *generation of hypotheses*. This ability is related to creativity. Research with older children indicates that creative children seem less concerned about error and are more willing to try out any possible idea.[13]

This research suggests some possible strategies for adults interested in developing creative children. Adult guidance that accepts children's experimenting with ideas, encourages "pretend play" and de-emphasizes "right" and "wrong" answers should encourage creativity. In the past, some preschool programs permitted children to experiment with materials like paint, clay, finger paint, and crayons as long as the children followed a few rules like "keep the paint on the paper." Even here, adults are tempted to push children toward such traditional standards, as painting the grass green. Even more damaging to the development of creativity is giving the children patterns or coloring books to get products more in keeping with adult standards. These patterns take the hypothesis-testing out of the experience and don't permit children to express their feelings and ideas. What could be an experience in developing creativity becomes an experience in following adult directions.

Adults can encourage creativity, as well as information-gaining, by asking questions in response to children's questions or problem situations the children face. In such situations, the children learn to formulate hypotheses. If one wheel of the wagon the children are pulling runs off the sidewalk and stops the wagon, the adult can lift the wagon back on the sidewalk; or the adult can ask the children why the wagon does not move and examine the wheels with them. This type of counterquestion is not possible in many situations, of course, and it requires more time and skill from the adult.

Developing Skill in the Tools for Education

To many adults, skills in reading, writing, and arithmetic are more important than the ability to think creatively, and some preschool children may be able to develop a fair degree of skill in reading, writing, and arithmetic during the preschool years. The authors, however, accept the point of view that these skills can be learned more efficiently when children enter the public schools.

Although they do not teach them directly, adults cannot ignore the abilities that are basic to the development of skill in these tools for education. To some degree, all children's spontaneous play involves language, which is related to reading, fine motor skills, which are related to printing and writing, and an understanding of quantity, which is related to arithmetic.

Interest in reading, fine motor coordination necessary for printing, and some understanding of quantity can be encouraged by planned activities for older preschool children. Some activities that encourage a desire to read are printing a report of a field trip while the children watch, printing labels for crayons and paper on the shelf, and printing the children's spontaneous stories or poems for them. Using puzzles also helps develop the form perception and fine motor coordination basic to printing. All types of art materials involve use of fine motor coordination. You can encourage math skills with counting games, such as how many cookies are needed to give one to each child at the table, and measuring activities, such as how much a child has grown or the distance between rows in the children's garden.

Planning a Program for Preschool Children

Even though the adult is aware of the skills children are developing and is eager to help them along, the authors consider the children's interests to be most important in curriculum planning for preschool children. Extensive discussion of program activities fall outside the domain of this book, however, and books that provide suggestions for activities are listed under supplementary references at the end of this chapter.

In this section, we do consider the implications that child development knowledge has for planning the day in the center. Large blocks of time without interruption enable children to select activities appropriate for their developmental level. This enables them to experience decision-making and helps them learn to pace themselves. Avoiding unnecessary interruptions, like requiring all the children to go to the bathroom at one time, encourages involvement in an activity and development of a longer attention span.

The period of the day devoted to free play permits the children to select from a wide variety of activities and to divide their time among these activities as they choose. In free play, however, children should not be permitted to misuse materials, such as building with books, nor to disrupt other children's activities. Children need to have the opportunity to select and plan from a wide variety of activities over a fairly long period of time—possibly about an hour. There should be opportunity for free play both indoors and out. In ideal weather, some of the indoor activities can be moved outdoors. Some materials, like blocks and puzzles, should be available every day. Others, like finger painting or specific table games, should be rotated from day to day.

Guidance in free play is not without problems. Some children have great difficulty in concentrating on an activity. Adults may have to spend more time sitting near and encouraging them to stick with an activity like a puzzle until it is finished. Some children are fearful about entering complicated social situations in the block corner or the doll corner. Starting to build blocks with a timid child and encouraging another child to join may be one way to help. Some children seem to be constantly interrupting others in what they are doing. Carefully watching these children in order to foresee conflicts and redirecting them before conflicts arise promote a more productive free play time.

Some adults are bothered by the amount of equipment on the floor and tables during free play time. The room may look better if children are required to return to the shelf one piece of equipment before getting another, but this requirement creates frequent interruptions from adult reminders and leads to less involved, less creative play. Children *should* be interrupted when they are destroying play equipment, however, as in throwing books or puzzle pieces. A warning that "clean-up time" is approaching and working with the children to put the playroom in order gives children a feeling of sharing responsibility for care of equipment.

Even though preschool children take the major responsibility for their learning, adults can make the difference between an environment that challenges and arouses children's interest in a variety of ideas and activities and one that permits random repetition of activities that are no longer interesting or useful. Children's developmental levels influence the amount of change and the number of planned activities for optimum learning. For younger preschool children, it is easy to provide too much equipment at one time, too many visitors, and too many field trips. Older preschool children, particularly those in a group with younger children, may tease and interrupt others because they have run out of ideas for constructive activities.

In planning special activities like cooking experiences, special visitors, and field trips, you need to think of children's developmental level, present interests, information and misinformation as evidenced through conversation, and their past experiences in the center and at home. Careful planning will assist the children's incorporation of new information through assimilation and accommodation.

Specially planned activities may be designed for the whole group or for individual children to pursue when interested, as in a learning center of books and pictures. Some group discussion with older preschool children is necessary to give them chances to get information from the adult and share their own ideas, but these discussion periods should be brief. Since sensory experiences are more important than words, specially planned experiences should emphasize displays, visitors, and field trips.

Even experienced professionals who know the children in their group cannot predict accurately how long they will be interested in a given topic. Many plans may be partially used or even eliminated entirely when children do not seem ready for an activity at a particular time. The children also provide clues as to how often to rearrange the room, change the science table, or remove some equipment and substitute something else. Chil-

dren seem to need a sameness in the appearance and routine of the center. A limited amount of change, as in rearrangement of equipment, can often begin a whole new group of activities.

The casual observer is likely to miss the planning that goes into an environment that encourages children to be responsible for their own learning. Parents are often impressed by situations where children sit still and listen for long periods of time. The evidence from recent research points to the noisy playroom as more conducive to learning that the discussion group where the adult talks and the children listen.[14]

Assessing Children's Development

Knowing what skills children are developing from month to month and whether they are making progress is essential to determining a program's effectiveness. Considering the limited staff time in most centers, planning how to collect the most important information requires thought.

A variety of checklists for evaluating children's progress is available, and several are noted in the books listed at the end of this chapter. Some checklists are too detailed to be used effectively in day care centers with limited staff. Choosing the areas that seem most important for individual children makes the task more manageable.

EVALUATING MOTOR AND LANGUAGE SKILLS

General health, motor skills, and language development can be evaluated more easily than thinking ability. Children who are rarely ill and capable of climbing to the top of the jungle gym and riding a tricycle may not require your attention in the area of health and motor skills. In the past, many programs weighed and measured all children at intervals, but comparing children with other children on height and weight is a relatively meaningless activity since they all vary in bone structure. If children lack appetite and energy for vigorous play, however, it would be helpful to know the increase in height and weight over a three- or six-month period.

Most important in evaluating fine motor skills and language is noting whether children use these skills in everyday activity. If children use language freely in communication with adults and other children, they are probably growing in language skills. Assessing children's understanding of language is more difficult. Questioning them is the best way to determine their understanding. This is another reason for talking with children whenever you can—at lunch time, getting up after nap, or waiting for a parent at the day's end. How much the children talk is more important than how many consonants they can pronounce correctly. Special problems of language development were noted in the section on language development in this chapter.

EVALUATING THINKING ABILITY

Evaluating children's motor and language skills is easy compared with evaluation of their thinking ability. As a worker in day care, you should have some understanding of the Intelligence Quotient (IQ) and how it is determined. Many parents and teachers have been overimpressed with the IQ because a specific number like 89 makes the IQ appear to be a precise measure. The IQ test assumes that, by observing some specific behaviors of children in a controlled situation, it is possible to determine what they know and make some prediction about their future learning potential.

It is difficult, even for a competent examiner specially trained to test young children, to determine what they know. Many preschool children are wary of strangers and may be uninterested in the tasks provided on the test. Using an IQ test such as the Stanford Binet assumes children have had equal opportunity to learn during their three, four, or five years of life. In reality, we know that opportunities to learn vary widely for infants and young children.

Certain children who seem to be having difficulty with learning may need to be referred to a psychologist for evaluation, which may include an IQ test. Frequently, such children are those suspected of having minimal brain damage. While it is important to identify them as early as possible, so that they can have special training, not all active, difficult-to-control children have minimal brain damage. Day-to-day observation of children in the center and, if possible, in the home is an essential supplement to more formal evaluations of thinking ability.

In spite of individual differences, growth during this period is rapid, and, to some extent, predictable. Awkward, uncertain, thirty-month-old children change to children who are so much more in control of their bodies that they can skip, suddenly change direction when running, and draw some recognizable figures, such as a stick figure of the teacher. Children who showed little understanding of yesterday and tomorrow now can discuss the fights they had with a friend last week or the trips they are going to take next week.

Glossary

Articulation   The learning of speech sounds and the rules for using these sounds.

Classification   Putting objects or events into categories of one or more dimensions, such as color or holidays.

Communication style   The unique way individuals use language to express thoughts and feelings and to clarify ideas.

Creativity   The willingness to engage in fantasy and in forming new hypotheses and the ability to use knowledge in original and constructive ways.

Generation of hypotheses Formation of "best guesses" about solutions to a problem.

Psycholinguists Those who study how the child uses the capacity to learn language in understanding and producing sounds and words.

Processing information Attending to features in the environment and organizing, evaluating, and manipulating concepts formed from these impressions.

Study Questions

1. Observe a three-year-old and a five-year-old child and compare them on:
   1. walking and running
   2. ability to hop and skip
   3. holding a paint brush
   4. putting together a puzzle
2. Record the words spoken by the three-year-old and the five-year-old during a five-minute period of free play.
3. Plan a learning experience that would help a four- or five-year-old child understand the concepts of "in" and "out."
4. Plan and carry out a thinking game with one or more preschool children. Record what you did and the children's responses. (Suggestions for thinking games can be found in Moore and Kilmer, *Contemporary Preschool Education: A Program for Young Children.*[15])

Notes

1. C. M. Davis, "Results of the Self-Selection of Diets by Young Children," *Canadian Medical Association Journal*, 41, 1939, p. 261.

2. E. H. Lenneberg, *Biological Foundations of Language*, Wiley, New York, 1967, p. 133.
3. D. McCarthy, "Language Development in Children," in *Manual of Child Psychology*, ed., L. Carmichael, Wiley, New York, 1954, p. 510.
4. R. Brown, *A First Language*, Harvard University Press, Cambridge, 1973, p. 271.
5. D. McNeil, "The Development of Language," in *Carmichael's Manual of Child Psychology*, ed., P. Mussen, Wiley, New York, 1970, p. 1101.
6. S. Stodolsky and G. Lesser, "Learning Patterns in the Disadvantaged," *Harvard Educational Review*, 37, 1967, p. 557.
7. B. Berenstein, "Social Structure, Language, and Learning," *Educational Research*, 3, 1961, p. 172.
8. Robert Hess and Virginia Shipman, "Parents as Teachers," ERIC Clearinghouse on Early Childhood Education, University of Illinois, 1967, p. 10.
9. W. Johnson, *Stuttering and What You Can Do About It*, University of Minnesota Press, St. Paul, 1961, pp. 110–111.
10. B. Wellman, I. M. Carse et al., *Speech Sounds of Young Children*, University of Iowa Studies Child Welfare No. 2, 1931, p. 35.
11. McCarthy, p. 549.
12. A. R. Luria, "The Role of Language in Formation of Temporary Connections," in *Psychology in the Soviet Union*, ed., B. Simon, Stanford University Press, Stanford, 1957, p. 116.
13. M. A. Wallach and N. Kogan, *Modes of Thinking in Young Children*, Holt, Rinehart & Winston, New York, 1965, p. 300.
14. David Elkind, "Misunderstandings about How Children Learn," in *Annual Editions Readings in Human Development* 1973–74, Dushkin Publishing Group, Guilford, Conn., 1973, p. 112.
15. S. G. Moore and S. Kilmer, *Contemporary Preschool Education: A Program for Young Children*, Wiley, New York, 1974, pp. 39–46.

Supplementary Readings

Croft, D., and R. Hess. *An Activities Handbook for Teachers of Young Children*. Houghton Mifflin, Boston, 1972.

Hess, R. D., and D. Croft. *Teachers of Young Children*. Houghton Mifflin, Boston, 1972.

Highberger, R., and S. Teets. "Early Schooling: Why Not?" *Young Children*, 29, 1974, 66–77.

Leeper, S. H., R. J. Dales et al. *Good Schools for Young Children*, 3rd ed. Macmillan, New York, 1974.

Seefelt, C. *A Curriculum for Child Care Centers*. Charles E. Merrill, Columbus, Ohio, 1974.

The Preschool Child's Relationships

6

After reading this chapter, you should be able to:

1. outline changing play behaviors with other children during the preschool period
2. suggest ways to help children learn to take turns and to control physical aggression
3. discuss modeling as a way of learning new behaviors
4. suggest possible reasons why the older preschool child seeks out adults rather than other children for companionship
5. describe characteristics that indicate a sense of initiative
6. describe factors you consider important in development of *conscience*
7. describe the family's influence on the child's behavior with other people

During the preschool period, relationships with other children are more important than they are during earlier periods of development. These relationships are influenced by past experiences in the family and in groups of children, by the children's skills, and by guidance from adults.

Changing Behaviors Due to Developmental Level

Children's skills in motor activity, language, and thinking ability influence their ability to participate in center activities with other children. Relating to other children involves the children's feelings about themselves and their regard for others of similar age and ability. Skills in relating to peers can affect relationships to others throughout life. Adults may overlook the importance of the children's developing social skills in their concern for their development of thinking skills, which appear to be more closely related to later success in school.

Between two and one-half years and the sixth birthday, children in a group usually spend more and more time in activities with each other. Increasing frequency of play with others generally increases the number of conflicts. Two causes for these conflicts are the inability of children of this age to plan ahead, and their inability to see a situation from another point of view.

The style of play also changes. The three-year-old often spends considerable time in solitary, onlooker, parallel, and associative play, as described in Chapter 3. In contrast, five-year-olds frequently participate in cooperative play with several other children around a central topic, such as building a fire station. At times, this type of play includes assigning jobs or roles like fire-engine driver. Such a project may continue over several days or longer.

Friendships between children change frequently during these years but are increasing in duration. Friends are more frequently selected from members of the same sex, possibly due to similarity in play interests and possibly due to the influence of older children and adult society. Now that a wider range of activities for both sexes, at home and in the center, is being encouraged, it may be that the number of same-sex play groups may change in the future.

AWARENESS OF RACIAL DIFFERENCES

Friendships during this period often involve children from different ethnic groups. Children are becoming increasingly aware of their ethnic identity. Many three-year-olds show an awareness of skin color in their response to racially different children.[1] In the past, black children, even during the preschool years, felt they were less valued because they were black. There is some evidence that black children now have a more positive image of themselves.[2] Since basic attitudes toward different ethnic groups are being formed at this age, a variety of races in both children and staff in a center is desirable. There is some evidence that positive experience with an individual of a different race encourages acceptance of people with different skin color at this age.[3]

SHARING

Acceptance of children from different ethnic groups is a concern to some adults, but many adults, including parents, are more concerned that children learn to share and work cooperatively with each other. Compared to other societies, we put great value on property rights and vigorously punish stealing.

As compared with toddlers, preschool children have a clearer concept of "mine," "yours," and what can be used by all the children in the center. Preschool children's attempts to take home attractive toys in their pockets or carry larger pieces of equipment out of the center, saying, "I brought it from home," indicate they do not share adult understanding of property rights. Making children feel guilty for these attempts to claim another's property is punishing them for their egocentricism, a normal part of being preschoolers. This egocentricism does not decline until the school years.[4]

Ability to abide by the rules of "taking turns" and asking other children for a "turn" becomes more a part of behavior during these years. This is really not true sharing, but an increasing ability to abide by adult rules. Children are better able to follow the rules because of past learning, increasing ability to remember, and greater facility with language. Conflicts over property are still frequent, especially if play materials are limited. One study showed that property was the most frequent cause of conflicts among preschool children.[5]

Praise for sharing and "taking turns" seems more appropriate guidance for this age than lengthy discussions on the importance of sharing. Modeling sharing behavior by both adults and other children is probably another important influence. In one experimental study, children who observed another child displaying a high frequency of sharing behavior showed a larger number of sharing behaviors than the control group who had not observed the model.[6]

SEX-ROLE LEARNING

Although ability to follow the rules for sharing behavior first emerges during this period, learning to meet expectations of what behavior is right for boys and what is right for girls has been going on since early infancy. The older preschool children are quite aware of being boys or girls and also aware of the genital differences between males and females. Traditionally, the nursery

schools have expected boys and girls to use the bathroom together, since it has been considered an opportunity to observe differences in genitals. Where parents can accept this practice, and in centers enrolling a large number of "only" children, sharing the bathroom seems a logical way to begin sex education.

Broadening the range of behaviors considered acceptable for males and females in our society was discussed in Chapter 4. The authors assume that most so-called masculine and feminine behaviors are not the result of biological differences. It appears to us that these behaviors are prescribed by the *culture* and that many of them are learned in early childhood. Parents have more influence than day care personnel in teaching sex-appropriate behaviors, and therefore parent values need to be considered in planning experiences for sex-role learning.

Learning about sex-appropriate behavior during the preschool years is influenced by adult attitudes (both verbal and nonverbal), modeling, planned experiences, and books. The attitudes of the adults were discussed in Chapter 4. The evidence for the influence of modeling was pointed up in discussion of sharing and will also be discussed in relation to aggression. When children can consider themselves members of a particular sex, they can relate to behaviors of other children as well as adults of the same sex. A center is fortunate that has on its staff both male and female workers who are capable of showing a range of behavior—physical affection and help, firm limit setting, and even the capacity to tighten the wheels on a tricycle. When this is not possible, volunteers can increase the range of models.

Older preschool children begin to show interest in what they will do when they grow up. Visiting male nurses, fire*women,* and female doctors are only a few of the visitors who can broaden children's concepts of the kinds of vocations open to both males and females.

One subtle but important way children are influenced in their perception of masculine and feminine behavior is through picture storybooks. There is growing evidence that picture books continue to show males more frequently and, when females are portrayed, they are more likely to be involved in domestic activities or passively watching the males.[7] By searching you can find some books that offer a different view of female characters. The book *Free to Be You and Me* provides a good basis for discussion with older preschool children.[8]

AGGRESSION

Aggression—physical and verbal attempts to hurt others and to destroy property—varies according to sex, with boys usually showing more aggressive behavior. Possibly this is due to greater adult acceptance of aggressive behavior in males.

Some change in the kind of aggression displayed can be expected as children come to the end of the preschool period. Their aggression can be expected to become more verbal (calling names like "stupid" and "dummy") and less physical (hitting, scratching, biting).

Helping children control their behavior without making them feel guilty about hostile feelings is a challenge to those who work with children. The adult's feelings may get in the way of viewing an aggressive episode objectively. Children's attempts at hurting other children remind us of our own desires to hurt others. The importance of skilled guidance is underlined by the fact that control of aggression seems to be one of the most important problems of our society. No one theory completely explains the causes of aggression, but three common causes are discussed here to help you plan for guidance in aggressive episodes.

Frustration. *Frustration* is defined as the barrier between individuals and their goals. Children may not always show aggression after frustration, especially if they are afraid of punishment. However, it seems safe to assume that there is a relationship between aggressive behavior and past or present frustration.

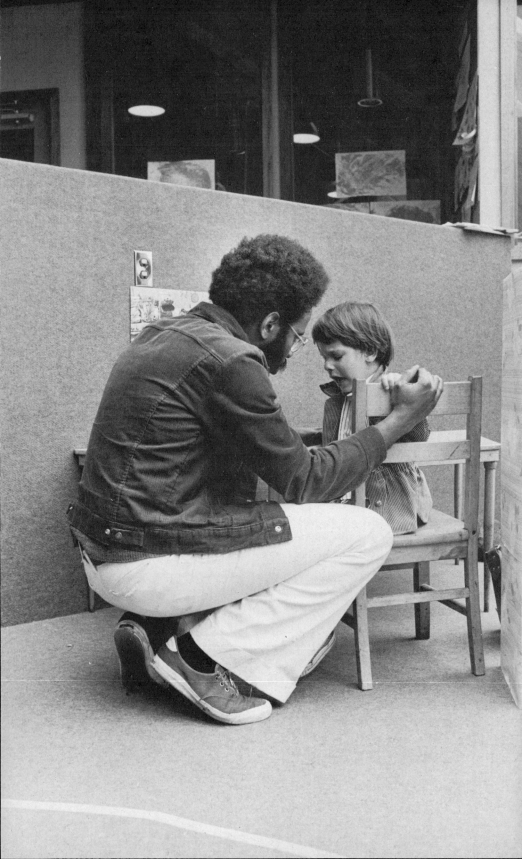

Opportunities for frustration in a day care center are numerous. One study found ninety goal-blockings per day for preschool children.[9] You can readily observe children frustrating other children. And adults are not always sensitive to the frustrations they cause in maintaining the routine of the center.

Everyone must learn to live with frustration, but the adult responsible for a group of children should periodically evaluate the number of frustrations children are experiencing. This is especially important when aggression is a continual problem.

Adults cannot change the maturity of individual children in their care, but alert guidance can prevent some frustration for other children. Keeping watch on children who are likely to get into conflict with other children and redirecting them to another activity when they look as though they were about to kick something down is one way. Setting clear rules and reminding children of them should eliminate some frustrations. Helping children talk out their feelings to each other helps them begin to see the other points of view and should help encourage language rather than fists to express hostile feelings.

Adults often cause unnecessary frustrations in carrying out the center's routine. Some of these are necessary, but in some centers many are not. Interrupting play activities without warning, making children wait for lunch or while others get ready for a field trip, and expecting children to sit still in a group for an uncomfortably long period are some of the most frequent unnecessary frustrations.

Helping children get rid of hostile feelings resulting from frustration in an acceptable way is another technique for reducing hurting behavior. Pounding nails with a hammer, working with soft clay or dough, finger painting, and vigorous running outdoors all seem to be particularly effective in draining off feelings in preschool children. Help children find activities that seem to help them work off angry feelings and relax. Then guide them to those activities when they seem too angry to control their behavior.

Modeling.   This is an important cause of aggressive behavior during the preschool years. Modeling was discussed in relation to sharing behavior, and in relation to adults providing an aggressive model when they spank. The research on aggression modeling is quite convincing. Observation of aggressive models seems sufficient to bring about that behavior in children.[10] Other children become increasingly important as aggressive models during the preschool years. You may have noted that one child who bites can start a rash of biting in a group of younger children.

Knowledge of modeling research provides a clue to how much adults should interfere in children's quarrels when hitting is involved. Since the more hitting children see the more likely they are to hit, reducing the amount of hitting they see should reduce the likelihood of their hitting to solve their problems. This means adult intervention and helping children solve the conflict through words. Modeling research also relates to techniques you suggest to children to protect themselves from the aggression of others. Telling children to hit back only increases the frequency of the behavior you are trying to discourage. Older preschool children are capable of learning to use language and physically remove themselves from an angry child's location to avoid being hurt.

Reward or reinforcement of aggression.   The third common cause for aggression was pointed up in one study that showed that moderately aggressive children increased their aggressive behavior over a period of months in a nursery school because they got what they wanted through aggression.[11] It takes an alert adult to realize when this is going on in a group. Some children do not protest when other children hit or take something from them. Encouraging children to hang on to toys if they had them first, and helping children tell others to stop pushing sets up the situation for all children to learn.

The amount of physical aggression you permit in a group of preschool children depends on your own values, the point of view of the administrators of the center, and the particular children in the group. Children who live in areas surrounded by physical violence must be able to defend themselves by using their bodies if necessary. Parents on the advisory board of the center can be helpful to staff in evaluating skills in self-protection needed in the home community.

To the authors, permitting or encouraging large amounts of physical aggression in a day care center because children must protect themselves at home does not seem a logical solution. The center may be one place where children can learn different ways of handling conflict. Preschool children make the distinction between home and center all the time in other areas of behavior such as eating and using the toilet. The significant factor in such cases is guidance to help the children avoid guilt feelings about hitting while they learn other methods for settling conflict.

Verbal aggression is different from physical aggression, and it requires different adult guidance. Freedom to find out what one's words do to other people may be an important part of the learning environment. Calling people "dumb" and "stupid" often hurts more, and has greater effect, than physical aggression. As children become less egocentric and more interested in other people, particularly other children, they learn from each other through these expressions of anger. At the same time, they are furthering their language development.

When the verbal aggression is directed toward adults, they can accept children's feelings with statements like "I know you're angry," without giving in if the conflict is over a limit on the children's behavior. In this interchange it is important to make children understand that it is acceptable to be angry. When the verbal aggression is directed toward other children, adults might listen without interfering until reversion to physical aggression seems likely. This gives the children a chance to solve conflicts independently.

Behavior with Adults

Children's behavior with adults is influenced by the adults' feelings and behavior. Preschool children make somewhat different demands on adults than younger children do. Older preschool children are quite capable of threatening the confidence you have in yourself. With experience, you learn to accept being called a "stinky" or a "dumb" teacher as the children's expression of unhappiness with something you have done, rather than as a threat to you as a person.

Some behaviors that are not threatening also make us angry, possibly because we were punished for the same behavior in childhood. Many of us are bothered by aggressive behavior, especially spitting and biting. Some of us are bothered by dependent, clinging children, while other adults prefer children who stay close and try to sit on laps at every opportunity.

You cannot change the kind of guidance you had as a child, but you can learn to be sensitive to the behavior that causes you to overreact. You can then be more thoughtful in handling situations involving that behavior. If you dislike children who cling, you can think twice before turning away children who want to sit on your lap. This lap sitting may be the way to begin a relationship with these particular children. Once you have established the relationship, you can help them toward independence.

DEPENDENCE

Dependence is the desire to be helped, comforted, and protected by others. Attachment, which is related to dependence, is a relationship focused on the main caregiver, in infancy.[12] The clinging behaviors shown in attachment and dependency are similar. Preschool children can be expected to be in the process of becoming independent, less dependent on adults, and more dependent on other children.

When children have just entered the day care

center—a strange situation to them—they can be expected to show more dependent behavior. Even with planning, some children may continue to focus on seeking adult help and attention. Research findings on the relationships between mothers' behavior and dependent behavior in children offer suggestions for adult planning. One study showed that mothers who consistently rewarded children's dependent behavior by responding to their demands for help and attention had more dependent children.[13] Reward alone does not seem to be sufficient explanation, however. Another study found that mothers who first punished dependent behavior, then gave in to the children's demands, had more dependent children.[14]

Observation suggests that children who show so much dependence on adults lose out on the experiences in the center, and parents and center staff should work out a plan for their guidance. The plan should involve praise, nonverbal at times (a nod or a smile is enough), each time the children attempt to be independent in playing alone or with others, in dressing or using the toilet independently. Some, but not all, requests for help and attention should be ignored. When adults do respond, the responses should be immediate, not some time after the children made the request. This type of guidance is not easy, especially with children who have become skillful in using whining to get adult attention.

Anxiety-producing situations are more likely to bring on dependent behavior.[15] In addition to reducing anxiety through gradual admission to the center, adults can help by following a similar routine from day to day, planning ahead with children for changes like field trips, and letting children know, when possible, that a favorite adult will be absent from the center. Another study showed that children made more demands on their mothers when the mothers were busy.[16] You may have noticed that some children make more demands for help and attention when adults are getting food on the table or putting down cots. In such situations, giving these children attention or a smile, nod, or eye contact *before* they ask for it may help diminish the behavior. At times, adults can give dependent children responsibility for helping in these routine chores. These jobs will take longer with children helping, but the children are getting attention for being responsible helpers.

INDEPENDENCE

Independence and self-reliance appear to be related to *achievement* behavior. Achievement is the children's attempt to obtain approval (and avoid disapproval) for competence in performance in situations where standards of excellence apply.[17] Achievement behavior has been studied more frequently in the area of intellectual mastery. Differences in achievement behavior are evident as early as the preschool years. One study showed that nursery school children who chose to spend more time in achievement activities sought less support and help from the staff and from mothers at home. Independence has been shown to be a consistent characteristic of children whose IQ scores increase.[18]

Our society places more emphasis on independence and achievement, particularly for males, than do many other societies. Considering the changing role of American women, dependence, independence, and achievement are as much a concern for females as for males.

Learning to be independent is only one factor in learning to be an achiever. Reward, punishment, and modeling of adults and older children, influence children's achievement behavior. Achievement behavior is significant because of its stability. Especially in the intellectual area, it is one of the most stable aspects of personality.[19] Many parents who want their children to succeed in school are concerned about it.

Personality Development and Self-Control

According to Erikson's theory, preschool children are establishing the sense of initiative.[20] This sense of initiative involves great expectations, with no concern for realistic evaluation of performance. One child, experimenting with sounds on the piano, replied to his mother's remark that some day he could take piano lessons with, "I know how to play the piano already." This statement shows a sense of initiative. By the time he is ready for piano lessons, he will be able to tell the difference between his "playing" and that of an adult.

A sense of initiative is based on basic trust, developed in infancy, and a sense of autonomy and positive self-concept, developed during toddlerhood. As outlined in Chapter 1, the sense of initiative involves the capacity to plan projects without concern for skills or materials in carrying them out. Forcing children to evaluate projects by adult standards may hinder their development of initiative. With age, children grow less positive in their self-evaluations, but at the preschool level, they should be encouraged to try many different kinds of activities, with no concern about failure.[21]

Helping children learn to live with the restraints imposed by society also influences their feelings about themselves. Statements like "People won't like you if you hit," and "You're a bad boy," hamper children's capacity to dream big and think well of themselves. Behaving acceptably should not be the only goal in guidance of preschool children.

DEVELOPMENT OF CONSCIENCE

Resisting temptation, evidence of guilt after doing something "wrong," and confession are behaviors that have been used in evaluating children's development of conscience. Adult guidance, the children's thinking ability, and their capacity to view a situation objectively seem to influence development of conscience. Of the three, adult guidance is the most important during the preschool years.

Parents are more important than center staff in this development, but research gives some guides for staff members. One fairly consistent finding is that parents who used physical punishment and removal of materials or privileges had children who rated lower on various measures of conscience.[22] More desirable techniques are giving the children reasons for changing their behavior or pointing out the effect on others of the children's behavior, because they provide information the children can use for future decisions about their behavior.

It appears that parents in families with low incomes may be more likely to use the power assertion techniques mentioned above, including spanking and other forms of physical punishment, more frequently than middle-class parents, because of the many pressures in their lives.[23] Children from such families may appear less sensitive to adult reasoning than middle-class children in the center. These are the children who may continue climbing on the fence after you have explained why this is not acceptable behavior. Such behavior can make you feel helpless and incompetent, and, in turn, you may be angry with the children for putting you in this position. In this frame of mind, it is easy to tell yourself that spanking is the only solution with such children. You may have to control yourself in order to teach the children self-control.

Day care staff can help some children learn to handle society's restrictions by helping them learn self-control. Here guidance that does not emphasize the adult's power is needed. Redirection to a different, interesting activity is a useful technique, but children who have difficulty controlling behavior may require some physical restraint. You may need to remove them from the fence and make them play indoors if they immediately go back to the fence. Often these children are very responsive to approval when they behave acceptably.

Relationships with parents also influence conscience development. Children who have warm, rewarding relationships with their parents are more likely to rate higher on conscience development. The need to develop a relationship with children before your approval or disapproval has meaning for them is evident the first day you work with a child or group of children. Until you know the children, you may have difficulty asserting a leadership role with them.

Developing a relationship is a highly individual matter and only general suggestions can help. If you can convey to the children your interest and concern and can show that you are usually consistent and therefore dependable, you will usually be well on the way to establishing a good relationship. As noted before, both children and adults have preferences for certain kinds of people. You can expect to develop a better relationship with some children than others. Children usually encounter several adults during the day in a center, and should develop a close relationship with one or two of them.

So far this discussion of conscience has assumed that a high rating for conscience development is desirable. Children do have to learn to control behavior sufficiently to live in a group without infringing on the rights of others. Some children, however, may be too concerned about making a mistake. You probably have observed children who seemed more concerned about adult approval than interested in trying something new. We should be pleased when these children break a few rules as long as they do not hurt other children.

A certain amount of testing of adult limits, such as making noise at naptime, is part of the children's education in self-control. This testing irritates the adult but it is a necessary part of the children's development of the feeling that they can exercise some control over what happens to them. When possible, experiencing the logical consequences of their behavior, such as resting in a room alone when they awaken several children in the nap room, helps them see the effect of their behavior without making them feel guilty about it. When you have to force compliance, as when children refuse to leave the playground at the time to go home, you can do it without making them feel they are "bad" because of their behavior.

GUIDANCE

To evaluate guidance you need to consider what children are feeling and learning. Use of reason instead of force gives children information and helps them feel they are responsible people rather than weak and helpless. This sense of self-control is encouraged if the adult will accept the limit-testing and, at the same time, prevent the children from hurting themselves and others. Reasoning, acceptance, and a warm relationship with at least one adult in the center contributes to the children's positive self-concept and sense of initiative.

Two other considerations in guidance should be mentioned here—modeling and consistency of adult demands. Modeling or copying behavior of adults and other children may be one of the most potent influences in the children's learning to fit with society's expectations. Adults, like children, have difficulty controlling their behavior when they are tired and angry. Being able to tell children you are sorry you handled them roughly when they were disturbing other children in the nap room can help them understand that adults get angry too, and it also sets an example for admitting mistakes.

Consistency in rewarding acceptable behavior and ignoring unacceptable behavior when possible has been pointed out in the research on behavior modification. In everyday work with children, however, consistency is not as easy or perhaps as desirable as it appears on the surface. The way children and adults feel and their ability to control behavior vary from day to day. Making exceptions to rules under special circumstances allows the adult to model sensitivity to the feelings of others. To avoid confusion when exceptions are made, adults should tell the children that an exception is made because they are tired or not feeling well. This verbalization helps children know what to expect in the future. In general, when expectations are similar from day to day children find it easier to live up to them.

"Time out" or isolation is a technique from behavior

modification that is used in some day care centers. While more appropriate for a preschooler than a younger child, isolation should be used with caution. It is a power assertion technique, in that the adult deprives children of the company of other children and play materials. The experience of being isolated probably arouses feelings of guilt and anger. Too many guilt feelings interfere with the children's developing a sense of initiative. Since sense of time is different in children and adults, children are often left too long in isolation. Even a period of five minutes can seem like a long time to children. Isolation in a locker or empty room is different from taking children to another room to talk or to pursue another activity when the children are upset. Helping children gain control by moving to another activity gives them the feeling that the adult is trying to help, not punish, them. "Time out," as used in behavior modification, should be used rarely, and only under guidance of a person who has had experience with the technique.

Influences on Social Relationships

As you note the differences among children in a group, it is easier to accept the variation if you can make some good guesses about the causes of the differences. Heredity is one important factor—it determines children's sex and, to a great extent, their appearance and size. Just how heredity affects the rate of development and of intelligence is not clear now, but it must play a significant role.

As far as social relationships are concerned, the environment reacts with the children's inherited characteristics from early infancy. By the time children are preschoolers, they have a background of experience with people who have reacted to their sexual identity, appearance, and skills. Differing behavioral expectations according to sex already have been mentioned. Also, large children usually have more demands made on them than do small children of the same age.

THE FAMILY

The family is an important influence on behavior variation, and one must look first at the cultural background. Certain values and ways of behaving are common to people who identify themselves as white middle class, poor white, poor black, black middle class, Mexican-American, or Indian. Some cultural groups encourage more competition than others. Some are less concerned about physical aggression. The adult who works with children from different cultural groups must learn the kind of behavior valued in the particular groups.

Another family factor that may affect the way children relate to other children and adults is whether the children are from one- or two-parent families. Many children in day care come from one-parent families, usually with the mother as the head. Father absence, whether temporary or permanent, has been studied frequently in relation to the effects on boys. The earlier in the children's life the father leaves home, the greater the influence on the children for both boys and girls.[24] Since fathers more frequently represent order and discipline in society, one might expect more problems in conscience development in father-absent families. Male workers in the day care center can be particularly helpful to these children in establishing self-control.

Ordinal position—whether the child is the oldest, middle or youngest child in the family—is another family influence on behavior. First children are more likely to be wanted, but their parents are more likely to convey their anxieties to these children.[25]

First children usually have more difficulty accepting new babies. You need to be prepared for marked changes in preschool children's behavior both when new babies come home from the hospital and later, when the babies are responsive and attracting the attention of the family and visitors. This is a time to accept the children's feelings, not tell them that they should love their baby brothers or sisters. At the same time, the children must be stopped if they take their anger out on younger children at the center.

As compared with the usual sibling relationships, twins have some unique problems. On the average, twins are slower in language development, probably because together they work out their own verbal and nonverbal communication system and see less need to communicate with others.[26] Some twins need help in establishing friendships with other children in a group. These same twins may be very successful in working together to tease or annoy adults and other children by knocking down block buildings or making noise at storytime. When possible, separating twins for part of the day at the center helps them establish themselves as individuals, not just parts of a team.

PAST EXPERIENCES IN GROUP CARE

The effects of experiences outside the home are even more difficult to evaluate than those in the home. Since few centers care for infants and preschool children, most information about earlier day care experience depends on parents' reports. One recent study indicates that children entering day care at ages two and three, as compared with children who remained at home, showed more distress at being separated from their mothers and more avoidance of strangers in an experimental situation.[27] A study of attachment in infancy reported no difference in attachment between home-reared infants and infants in day care.[28]

Whether children can adjust to day care more easily when they begin the experience in infancy remains to be determined. The number of different day care arrangements children have experienced, whether or not they have had the opportunity to adjust gradually to these arrangements, and the quality of relationships established probably would affect the degree of anxiety they experience in separation from their parents.

Neither parents or center staff find it easy to accept crying when the parents leave in the morning if the children have been in the center for six months or more. This behavior may be expected in some children, and the cause may be the simple one that children, like adults, have days when they would rather stay in bed than go out to face the world. Or, it may show the children's uncertainty about their relationship to their families and others. Crying children who have made the initial adjustment to the center usually have to leave their mothers, but they should be encouraged to express their feelings. Telling them to stop crying or implying that they are "babies" or "sissies" may make them feel there is something wrong or unworthy in their feelings.

Evaluating Children's Relationships

Behavior variation, such as sudden appearance of separation anxiety, makes assessing children's relationships more difficult than evaluating other skills. Behavior with other children varies more from day to day than do such skills as climbing or cutting with scissors. Relationships with others are affected by changes in the children's lives, like birth of a sibling, absence of a father due to a new job, or a move to a new home.

To evaluate children's behavior with others, observation records over a period of time are needed. Age and past experiences must be considered, as well as current experiences in the center and at home. This kind of evaluation is necessary to help adults see more objectively what behaviors they may be encouraging. It may be that proper evaluation can help parents and center staff work to reduce behaviors that interfere with the children's relationships with others.

During this period the child is working toward the following competencies:

1. selecting an activity and following the activity through to completion
2. directing requests for attention increasingly toward other children rather than adults
3. using verbal means for expressing anger instead of hitting, biting, or destroying other children's products
4. playing cooperatively with one or more children but also able to play alone
5. incorporating center rules and standards for behavior and following adult directions most of the time
6. planning and carrying out projects with others
7. showing confidence that children and adults will accept them and that they can cope with new situations (positive self-concept)

This list of competencies can serve as a reminder of the variety of social skills and the children's feelings about themselves that develop during the preschool years. These feelings about self and social skills change throughout life. The foundation laid down during the preschool years eases the move from family and center caregivers into the childhood community during the elementary school years.

Glossary

Achievement Efforts made to obtain approval and avoid disapproval for competence in situations where standards of excellence apply.

Aggression Verbal (ridiculing) or physical (hitting) behavior directed toward injuring another person.

Culture Set of customs and learned behavior in a particular group of people.

Dependence Desire to be helped, comforted, and protected by others.

Frustration A barrier that prevents individuals from getting what they want. This barrier may be another individual, an object, or the individuals' own lack of skill.

Ordinal position Determined by order of birth in the family.

Social class Division of society into groups according to education, occupation, and income level of the head of the family.

Study Questions

1. Observe a group of preschool children during a half hour's free play indoors, preferably with blocks or in housekeeping corner. Record the number of children who leave and the number who join the group. Record also the themes or topics for play—building airports, making pies, etc.

2. Describe the fights or conflicts in a group of children during a thirty-minute period. (This can be observed more easily indoors.) Indicate your hypotheses regarding the cause or possible causes for these conflicts.

3. If possible, observe a child's first day with a group of children. Observe again a week later, noting outstanding differences in behavior.

4. Observe in a day care center for an hour, recording the behavior you liked and the behavior that irritated you. Analyze why you think you felt this way about these behaviors.

5. Observe a boy or girl around age three and another child of the same sex around age five. Note the number of times each child tried to get help or attention from adults.

6. Observe, for at least an hour, a child who is considered aggressive by the day care center staff. For each aggressive episode, note whether the child achieved his or her goal.
7. Observe a child you consider a mature five-year-old. Give evidence from your observation of the child's range of success in accomplishing the seven competencies listed at the end of this chapter.
8. Observe a staff member in a day care center for an hour. If possible, describe one use of a power assertion technique, one use of reasoning, and one situation in which the adult served as a model of acceptable behavior.

Notes

1. H. W. Stevenson, "Studies of Racial Awareness in Young Children," in *The Young Child: Reviews of Research*, ed. W. W. Hartup and N. L. Smothergill, National Assn. for the Education of Young Children, Washington, D.C., 1967, p. 211.
2. A. T. Soares and L. M. Soares, "Self Perception of Culturally Disadvantaged Children," *American Educational Research Journal*, 6, 1969, p. 42.
3. Stevenson, p. 207.
4. Jean Piaget, *Science of Education and the Psychology of the Child*, Orion Press, New York, 1970, p. 176.
5. H. C. Dawe, "Analysis of Two Hundred Quarrels of Preschool Children," *Child Development*, 5, 1934, p. 149.
6. W. W. Hartup, "Peer Interaction and Social Organization," in *Carmichael's Manual of Child Psychology*, ed. P. Mussen, Vol. II, 3rd ed., Wiley, New York, 1970, p. 423.
7. Kathy Barber, *Sex Role Behaviors in Selected Children's Literature in 1960–65 and 1970–71*, Unpublished master's thesis, University of Tennessee, Knoxville, 1973, p. 33.

8. F. Klagsburn, Ed. *Free to Be You and Me*, McGraw-Hill, New York, 1974.

9. C. L. Fawl, "Disturbances Experienced by Children in Their Natural Habitats," in *The Stream of Behavior*, ed., R. G. Barker, Appleton, New York, 1963, p. 103.

10. A. Bandura and A. C. Huston, "Identification as a Process of Incidental Learning," *Journal of Abnormal and Social Psychology*, 63, 1961, p. 317.

11. G. R. Patterson, R. A. Littman, and W. Bricker. "Assertive Behavior in Children: A Step Toward a Theory of Aggression," *Monographs of the Society for Research in Child Development*, 32, 1967, p. 23.

12. R. R. Sears, "Attachment, Dependency, and Frustration," in *Attachment and Dependency*, ed. J. L. Gewirtz, V. H. Winston, Washington, D.C., 1972, p. 23.

13. J. Kagan and H. A. Moss, *Birth to Maturity: A Study in Psychological Development*, Wiley, New York, 1962, p. 214.

14. R. R. Sears, E. E. Maccoby, and H. Levin, *Patterns of Child Rearing*, Harper & Row, New York, 1957, p. 171.

15. M. K. Rosenthal, "The Effect of a Novel Situation and Anxiety on Two Groups of Dependency Behavior," *British Journal of Psychology*, 58, 1967, p. 363.

16. R. R. Sears, "Dependency Motivation," in *Nebraska Symposium on Motivation*, ed. M. Jones, Lincoln: University of Nebraska Press, 1963, p. 54.

17. V. C. Crandall, "Achievement Behavior in Young Children," in *The Young Child: Reviews of Research*, ed. W. W. Hartup and N. L. Smothergill, National Assn. for the Education of Young Children, Washington, D.C., 1967, p. 165.

18. *Ibid*, p. 170.

19. H. A. Moss and J. Kagan. "The Stability of Achievement and Recognition Seeking Behaviors," *Journal of Abnormal and Social Psychology*, 62, 1961, pp. 504–513.

20. E. H. Erikson, *Childhood and Society*, 2nd ed., Norton, New York, 1963, p. 273.

21. P. Katz and E. Zigler, "Self-Image Disparity: A Developmental Approach," *Journal of Personality and Social Psychology*, 5, 1967, p. 186.

22. M. L. Hoffman, "Moral Development," in *Carmichael's Manual of Child Psychology*, ed. P. Mussen, Vol. II, 3rd ed., Wiley, New York, 1970, p. 285.

23. Hoffman, "Moral Development," p. 293.

24. E. Hetherington and J. Deur, "The Effects of Father Absence on Child Development," in *The Young Child: Reviews of Research*, ed. W. W. Hartup, Vol. II, National Association for the Education of Young Children, Washington, D.C. 1972, p. 317.

25. J. A. Clausen, "Family Structure, Socialization, and Personality," in *Review of Child Development Research*, ed. L. Hoffman and M. Hoffman, Vol. II, Russell Sage Foundation, New York, 1966, p. 16.

26. D. McCarthy, "Language Development in Children," in *Manual of Child Psychology*, ed. L. Carmichael, Wiley, New York, 1954, p. 561.

27. M. C. Blehar, "Anxious Attachment and Defensive Reactions Associated with Day Care," *Child Development*, 45, 1974, p. 690.

28. B. M. Caldwell, C. M. Wright et al., "Infant Day Care and Attachment," *American Journal of Orthopsychiatry*, 40, 1970, p. 411.

Supplementary Readings

Baker, K. R. *Ideas That Work with Young Children*, National Association for the Education of Young Children, Washington, D.C., 1972.

Leeper, S. H., R. J. Dales, D. S. Skipper, and R. L. Witherspoon. *Good Schools for Young Children*. Macmillan, New York, 1974.

Read, K. *The Nursery School*. W. B. Saunders, Philadelphia, 1971.

7

Parents and Staff Working Together

After reading this chapter, you should be able to:

1. discuss the importance of a good parent-staff relationship
2. describe ways to build a relationship with parents
3. discuss ways in which parents influence their children
4. discuss advantages and disadvantages of the various means of communicating with busy parents
5. evaluate the parents' position as decision-makers of the center's policies

Traditionally, parents have been excluded from decision-making positions about the care and education of their children. The school has been a leader in this pattern of exclusion, often walling off the parents, suggesting that the professionals were in control and the nonprofessionals should stay out.

Parents have stayed out perhaps because they felt unqualified to come in. *Newsweek* quotes Harvard psychologist Burton White as saying, "The vast majority of educated women in this country don't know what the hell they are doing when they have a child. We just don't prepare our women or our men for parenting."[1] And lower-income, less well-educated parents have been given little if any consideration in this matter. Often women have learned breathing exercises to prepare themselves for labor and delivery of a baby, but have learned nothing about how to encourage motor or language development in infants, toddlers, and preschool children.

Rationale for Parent Participation

Federally supported preschool programs have emphasized the importance of good parent-teacher relationships. Project Head Start and Title IV-A Day Care Centers have been leaders in the area of parent participation in decision-making positions. Fortunately, other agencies that serve children are also beginning to serve the parents. One way to do this is to allow parents more control over the lives and educations of their children.

Parent participation in Head Start programs is mandatory. The Policy Manual specifically calls for establishment of Policy Councils that have the following responsibilities, among others: to participate in the selection of the Head Start Program Director and to help establish criteria for the selection of other staff personnel; to hear complaints about the program and to make suggestions for improvements, to help organize activities for parents and encourage parent participation in the program.[2]

In many states, Title IV-A Day Care Centers were bound in their contracts to involve the parents by establishing a *Parent Policy Council* that shares in the decision-making process of the day care center.

According to Robert Hess and his associates, "The rationale for parent participation in decision-making is based on the belief that people will not be committed to decisions in which they had no involvement. Furthermore, it is believed that the processes of considering information, decision-making, and implementation are, in themselves, educational and aid in developing leadership skills. It also is argued that parents know their own situations best, and hence must be involved in planning for their children's education."[3]

Understanding Parents' Feelings about Day Care

REASONS FOR SEEKING DAY CARE

Parents seek day care facilities for their young children for a variety of reasons. In many cases, the one-parent family is the reason: the mother, raising the children alone, must work outside the home in order to have a regular income. She must make arrangements for care for her children. In other cases, widowed or divorced women who receive social security benefits or alimony and child support payments find that rising inflation means that they cannot live on their fixed incomes. They, too, must go to work and they seek child care facilities. Sometimes one-parent families are headed by fathers who, because of the death or divorce of their wives, are attempting to raise their children alone. They, too, are in need of day care facilities.

In addition to children from one-parent families, many children have mothers and fathers who both work, either by choice or by necessity. And occasionally children who live with relatives other than their parents, with friends or perhaps in a foster home, are placed in day care. Centers may also be used to provide an outlet for children who live in unusual home situations such as with physically or mentally handicapped parents or siblings.

For whatever reason parents enroll their children in day care, we can be sure that they will be searching for high quality facilities and will come to the day care center with some questions and anxieties.

PARENTS' CONCERNS ABOUT DAY CARE

Parents' feelings about day care are mixed. They need and yet fear the center's facilities. Most often, they are concerned about the quality of care their children will receive, the possible lack of individual attention, their own feelings of guilt, and their children's development of attachment to others. Let's take a closer look at these worries.

The first day care centers and even many of those in existence by the end of World War II left much to be desired in the way of meeting all the needs of children. Many parents remember, or have their own parents or friends to remind them, of these less-than-desirable facilities.

One big complaint about the early (and some present) day care centers is the fact that many children are cared for by few workers who do not take a personal interest in them. Therefore, parents are concerned that their children may be just parts of the group and not treated as individuals.

Guilt feelings about leaving their children are seen in many parents and seem to be especially evident in those mothers who work by choice rather than by necessity. Bruno Bettleheim has labeled this feeling *maternal guilt*. He suggests that it has its origin in the unfounded and often unspoken belief that a truly "good mother" will find complete satisfaction in a life of devotion to her home and family.[4]

Added to the guilt are mixed feelings about attachments children may form in the center. Parents want their children to like their teachers and to be happy in the day care program, yet they do not want their children to become too attached to other adults, who then would come between parents and children.

In addition to parental worries, mutual fear is also involved in the parent-staff relationship. Strange as it may seem, parents and staff often fear each other. Both feel somewhat threatened by each other and the relative positions they will have in relationship to the children. As a member of the teaching staff, you must accept the fact that whenever people meet in a new situation there will be some fear and anxiety. If you understand the parents' negative feelings, you can help to reduce them. Often poorer, less well-educated parents have a fear of the "school" building and the teachers. They resist going into the building and hesitate to communicate with the teachers.

The day care staff can help parents feel secure about leaving their children in the center. This can be accomplished only if teachers and parents have warm personal relationships, built upon mutual respect and confidence.

Establishing the Relationship

When parents and children come to the center for the first time, the parents usually have some specific expectations of what they will find. Although expectations vary with each parent, they will become evident to the teacher as parents begin to comment and ask questions.

If you are prepared for the parents' questions, you will be able to give more thorough, accurate answers. Typically, parents begin by asking what the hours of the center are and when it is closed for holidays or vacations. Next comes the financial question of tuition fees, along with the ages of children served and if space is available. Usually parents will want to know the qualifications of the director and staff, along with the average adult-child ratio and the extent of expected and allowed parent participation. Some parents will question the philosophy and goals of the program, specifically, the methods of discipline and provision for individual attention for each child.

If parents want to discuss specific information about their children, wait until the children can be involved in activities with other children or other adults. It is never a good policy to talk about children in the children's presence.

While the children are absent, you as the teacher may also have questions to ask. Without seeming to pry into the parents' privacy, you will want to obtain information about the children's ages, home life situations, siblings, health histories, and general physical, mental, and emotional development from birth to the present. You will want to know if the children have previously been enrolled in child care facilities and if they have been cared for on a regular basis by caregivers other than their parents.

After a brief visit and a look around the facilities, you may suggest that parents return another day to discuss other enrollment details and to fill out the necessary registration forms. Discuss the possibility of gradual admittance to the day care center, perhaps allowing children to come half a day for a few days until they seem ready to spend the whole day without their parents. A booklet that will answer questions on the center's operating policies may be given to parents. It should not be used in place of direct communication, but as a supplement and a reference source.

All center staffs will want to create their own booklets,

covering material specifically important to them. The following information may be included: Name, address, and phone number of the center, chairperson of the board of directors, chairperson of the parents' advisory committee, director, and each teacher. Hours during which the center is open. Holidays on which the center is closed. Payment of fees. Items to be brought by children (paint shirt, sheet and blanket, extra change of clothes). Policy section (toys from home, meals, naps, reporting absent children, giving medicine at the center, sick children, late parents, withdrawing from the center).

The booklet should fit the needs of the parents, teaching staff, and children. It should answer many of the parents' questions and most importantly, it must be written on a level the parents can understand. Make it short, interesting, and illustrated. Plan for it to be an enjoyable experience both in preparation and presentation.

Once the decision has been made to enroll children in the center, teacher and parents can begin to develop their relationship. As a professional day care worker, you will need to consider children as products of their environments, their homes. Be aware that their parents' past, present, and future circumstances shape this environment.

Parents too are shaped by their environment. A day care center may serve a variety of parents who are in a variety of situations, with a wide range of income and education levels. You may have parents who are professional workers, technicians, laborers, and unemployed. Each parent must be considered individually, as a unique, important person. Day care workers must be as concerned with each parent as with each child in the center.

Communicating with Parents

The teaching staff must take the initiative in communications, to make the parents feel secure, worthwhile, and welcome. There are many ways to keep the lines of communication open.

BRIEF CHATS

These are important to parents, teachers, and children. The informal exchanges of greeting and information do much to build the relationship between parents and teachers. However, they must be kept brief because parents should not be held too long. Also, the teacher must be available to greet other children as they arrive for the day and therefore must not become involved in long conversations.

NEWSLETTERS

Parents like newsletters. They are relatively simple to prepare and distribute and are well worth the effort. A newsletter may be a one-page, mimeographed sheet or a several-page booklet. It may be printed weekly, bimonthly, or monthly. Its content is as variable as the people who prepare it.

One center in Kentucky printed a weekly page called *The Play Yard News*. In it, the teacher summarized what had happened during the week, including exciting events that occurred (such as the birth of five baby hamsters), visitors, birthdays, and special notices to parents. A copy of this newsletter was safety-pinned to each child's clothing every Friday afternoon.

A center in Tennessee chose to print a sophisticated bimonthly report that ran regular columns written by the center's staff. The director wrote to the parents about things of general concern and happenings to the center as a whole, including such things as a reminder of holidays, operating policies, number of enrollment, and openings in each age level group. Individual teachers wrote of such specific incidents in each group as birthdays, visitors, and field trips. In addition, the newsletter used a regular column from the cook, giving a recipe for something the children had enjoyed for lunch, or one that the children could help to prepare (such as a Jell-O fruit salad).

One paragraph was designated for each of the following topics: art activity (such as play dough with the recipe included); singing activity (with the words of a new song); finger plays (with words and actions); story time (five suggested books available on loan from the day care or local library); the next unit topic (such as Colors Are Fun); and toys are free (instructions on how to make an educational toy from such home waste materials as milk carton blocks).

These newsletters were placed on a table in the entrance hall of the center. As parents picked up their children, they also picked up copies of the newsletter. The director reported that the parents talked of how they enjoyed and appreciated receiving the newsletter.

SHORT NOTES

These can be safety-pinned to children's clothing and serve as an excellent means of occasional parent-teacher communication. Such notes are especially useful for a teacher who may not see some children's parents—sometimes someone else picks up the children or, on a staggered staff pattern, one teacher may leave in the afternoon before the children leave. One mother reported her pleasure at finding the following note attached to her four-year-old son's shirt: "Dear Ms. Holder, Today Frankie fingerpainted. He chose his own colors and certainly seemed to enjoy the experience. He asked to have his picture put on the wall but he will be bringing it home in a few days. Just thought you would enjoy knowing of this 'first' for Frankie. Sincerely, Ann Prast." The teacher's enthusiasm for the child certainly came through, and the mother appreciated it.

Notes from parents may keep the teacher from having to guess about what is bothering children. Mr. Keys sent his son Kevin with the following note: "Dear Miss Pat, I had several emergency calls last night and unfortunately Kevin was awakened. If he seems cross today, it may be because he is tired. I am sorry. Keith Keys."

TELEPHONE CALLS

Calls can be very reassuring and show the teacher's concern for the feelings of parents as well as children. One morning just as two-year-old Sarah entered the center, she began to scream and cry. Her mother and teacher tried to comfort her, but she could not calm down. The mother, who had to go to work, was most upset at her daughter's distress. She left, also in tears. The teacher held and talked to Sarah. Soon Sarah made her teacher understand that she had wanted to bring her doll to the center that day, but had left her sitting on the floor of her room. The teacher assured Sarah that the doll would be safe at home and that she could bring her another day. She suggested that Sarah might enjoy playing with a new puzzle the center had just been given. Sarah agreed, and they went together to the puzzle table. Later in the morning, the teacher called Sarah's mother to tell her of the child's problem and her present condition. The mother, greatly relieved, appreciated the teacher's interest and thoughtfulness for her and her child.

Brief phone calls also may be used to relay messages, clear up misconceptions, request meetings, reassure parents, check on ill or absent children, and generally show teacher concern. The telephone is a wonderful invention. Don't save it for emergency use only.

And be prepared to have parents call you, both at the center and at home. Again, these conversations can be kept short and still provide warmth and understanding to concerned parents. One day care worker reported that a mother called her at home every evening for two weeks, always at supper time. The mother began her conversation by saying that Billy (who was enrolled at the center) wanted to talk with his teacher. Billy talked a few minutes and then the mother took over, usually with questions about cooking or child care techniques. However, at the end of the two weeks, she stopped calling but did talk with the worker when she picked Billy up at the center.

PARENT-INITIATED MEETINGS

Purposes for parent-teacher meetings can vary. Sometimes parents may want to discuss their children, or the center. Other meetings may deal with home economic problems or personal needs of the parents. Work meetings may be scheduled during which sewing, mixing paints, making play dough, cleaning, and general repair work may be done at the center.

One type of meeting that has consistently met with success, as indicated by a high percentage of attendance, is the *parent-initiated meeting*. That is to say, the parents think of the idea, make all of the arrangements, conduct, and evaluate the meeting. These are definitely parents' meetings. They are not teachers' meetings with parents attending. And they do provide excellent opportunities for parent-teacher interaction. Having the center's cook prepare a picnic type of supper, when possible, may be an added treat.

Late-afternoon meetings seem to be convenient for many parents and, of course, their children will be cared for in the center either by other paid workers or the regular teachers on a rotating basis. Although this type of gathering may be difficult to arrange, it has proven to be a valuable method for parents and teachers to get to know each other.

FATHER'S DAY SPECIAL

Too often society seems to minimize both the responsibilities and the rights of the fathers concerning their children. The tendency has been to eliminate or bypass fathers. Even in their first moments of fatherhood, they have generally been excluded. They have not been permitted to be present at their children's births or to touch their children until mothers and babies are released from the hospital. Perhaps the closed delivery-room door and the nursery window glass have created a barrier between fathers and children that has too long been accepted, and even expected.

Fortunately, many fathers now are rejecting this detached role; they are insisting on involvement. Day care staff should make it as convenient as possible for fathers to come to the center. Make them feel welcome and needed. Plan a special day for fathers to visit. A Saturday session is best, although a holiday or evening session may also be appropriate. Children can attend as usual (without fee) and fathers can come to observe their children's daily activities.

Mr. Sams attended for several hours, watching and playing with his five-year-old daughter Betty. Obviously both were delighted with his presence. "You have made me feel part of my child's learning and I want to do something for you. I'm not a rich man, but I am real good at mixing cement and digging holes. Next Saturday I'm coming down here and I'm going to set those tires in the ground so all the children can climb on them," Mr. Sams told the teacher. (Tires set this way make excellent crawling and climbing toys.)

Most fathers are concerned about their children's care. They must have the opportunity to share in the daily care and in decision-making. Teachers should expect, although not insist upon, father participation.

The children in your program who do not have fathers living at home also must be considered. If many of your children come from mother-only homes, you probably would not attempt a Father's Day Special. You could modify this idea to include both fathers and working mothers, who, because of their schedules, cannot visit the center during regular operating hours.

The mere idea of parent-teacher conferences may create anxiety for parents, teachers, and children. If there is one thing that is *not* needed between these groups, it is anxiety. Perhaps parents remember back when they were in school, when their parents went to school to talk with their teachers. Too often these structured, formal meetings meant trouble. Teachers must work with parents to build a personal, nonthreatening relationship in which either may request a conference.

The traditional form letter ("Dear Mr. and Mrs. James, It is time for our semiannual conference. Please come to my room on April 14 at 4:00 to discuss your child's progress. Sincerely, Mrs. Smith") has no place in the day care center's parent-teacher relationship. Possibly it should also be eliminated from all other parent-teacher arrangements, for it discourages open communication and puts barriers between the adults who care for children.

A more acceptable request for a conference may be a handwritten note: "Dear Ms. James, I have really enjoyed talking with you as you bring and pick up John at the center. I am glad that we have these few minutes for quick chats. I would like to have a little longer period to talk with you about John's adjustment to the day care program. Would it be possible for you to meet with me here at the center on Thursday, April 14 at 4:00? John could play in the yard with Ms. Sneed. I will call you on Monday to see if this is convenient. If it is not, we will try to work out a better time. I am looking forward to seeing you. Sincerely, Jane Smith."

The manner in which conferences are arranged and carried out will have an impact on their outcomes. The stereotyped, teacher-lecture-the-parents-for-fifteen-minutes procedure must not be part of the parent-teacher relationship in the day care center. Ideally, long before a conference is held, the adults will have established a sharing relationship.

INVITATIONS

Special parties or celebrations often attract parents to the center. Even working parents may be able to arrange for an afternoon off in order to attend a birthday or Halloween party. However, it has been the authors' experience that no parents, of whatever background, respond well to a mass-produced, fill-in-the-blank type of invitation. Response is better to handwritten invitations, if each is followed with a personal, spoken invitation or phone call. The teacher should not pressure parents to attend. Children of parents who do not attend should not be excluded from any of the activities. On the contrary, children whose parents are not present should be given special teacher attention so that they do not feel left out.

Invitations to special occasions should include assurance to parents that their children will be well cared for whether or not the parents are able to attend. Such parties should provide a pleasant experience for all the children, parents, and teachers. Certainly they provide a good opportunity for parent-teacher communication.

OPEN HOUSE

Often the informality of an open house setting will bring parents to the center. They can come and go, casually, see the facilities, meet other parents, and visit with the staff. Sunday afternoons usually are the best time for such activities. Again, handwritten notes, followed with verbal, personal contact, may encourage parents to attend.

Often local townspeople who are interested in the center may visit during an open house, although they have no personal need of its services. These people may be a great source of potential support within the community and may have many experiences and services to share with the center staff and children. Have visitors sign a guest book with their names and addresses. This list can provide potential resource people.

PHOTOGRAPHS

Occasionally, parents and staff find that direct communication is rarely possible. If there are long intervals between personal contacts, a photograph album of center activities may help bridge the communication gap. The photographs can show children participating in regular daily activities as well as in special events.

The album should include pictures of all children, staff, volunteers, special visitors, center pets, etc. It can be taken home where the parents can look at the picture and have their children tell them the story of what is happening. This involves the parents in the center's activities, introduces them to their children's friends and teachers, and provides a learning experience for all.

Even if the day care center has limited funds, such a project may be possible. Many high schools and vocational schools have photography departments that will process the film for the cost of materials, which are very inexpensive.

A collection of slides can bring the center alive to parents. This is an excellent way to show what's happening at the center. An accompanying cassette tape can be an on-the-spot recording or a commentary added later. Watching and listening, parents and children together can enjoy the events that take place at the center as well as spend time talking together.

The staff must make certain that a slide projector or viewer and tape player are available to lend to parents who do not have these items in their homes. Also, arrangements may be made to show the slides at a parent-staff group meeting.

There are many ways to communicate with parents. We have suggested some, and you will think of many more. It is impossible to say that one method is more effective than another, because each parent, center, and community is unique.

You will need to evaluate your particular situation, consider the needs of the parents you are trying to communicate with, and choose what seems to you the most likely means to success. You may use several different methods in an attempt to reach as many parents as possible.

The attitude of the staff is more important than the particular method used. If the staff lacks interest and enthusiam, if they do not see the importance and value of home-center relations, their efforts will fail.

Communication between parents and staff members is vitally important because both are caregivers of the children. Day care centers are designed not to relieve parents of their responsibilities, but to help develop them within themselves and their families. Parents and staff together share the responsibility and the joy of raising the generations of tomorrow.

Glossary

Maternal guilt Some mothers' bad feelings toward themselves for not living up to certain expectations, such as remaining at home to care for their children.

Parent education Staff and parents working together, trying to improve parenting techniques and increase parental knowledge.

Parent-initiated meeting Meeting held at the request of parents or organized entirely by parents.

Parent involvement Staff and parents working together, with parents directly or indirectly involved in all aspects of the program including decision-making positions.

Study Questions

1. Compare the relationship of parents and teachers when you were a child in elementary school to the present-day relationship of the parents and teachers of day care center children.

2. Discuss the importance of having parents who are concerned with and supportive of the day care program.
3. Arrange for a panel of parents to come to your class and discuss their interest in making decisions that affect their children.
4. Discuss possible problems that may arise when parents are involved in the decision-making process of the day care center.
5. Compare a day care child's relationship with his or her parents to that child's relationship with his or her teacher.
6. Ask the director of a local day care center to come to your class and describe the center's most successful methods of communicating with parents.

Notes

1. "Never Too Young To Learn," *Newsweek*, May 22, 1972, p. 94.
2. *Head Start Policy Manual*, Part B, Section B-2, U.S. Dept. of Health, Education & Welfare, Office of Child Development, Washington, D.C., 1970, p. 3.
3. Hess, R., M. Bloch, J. Costello, R. Knowles and D. Largay. "Parent Involvement in Early Education," in *Day Care: Resources for Decisions,* E. H. Grotberg ed., Washington, D.C.: Office of Economic Opportunity, 1971, p. 277.
4. Bruno Bettelheim, "Child Rearing," in *Annual Editions Readings in Human Development* 1973–74. Dushkin Publishing Group, Guilford, Conn., 1973, p. 188.

Supplementary Readings

Hymes, J. L., Jr. *Effective Home School Relations.* Southern California Assn. for the Education of Young Children, 1974.

Karnes, M. *A New Role for Teachers: Involving the Entire Family in the Education of Preschool Disadvantaged Children.* University of Illinois, Urbana, 1969.

Lundberg, C., and V. Miller. "Parent Involvement Staff Handbook: A Manual for Child Development Programs." Mississippi Head Start Training Coordinating Council, Jackson, Miss., 1972.

Samuels, S. "Johnny's Mother Isn't Interested." *NEA Journal*, 62, February, 1973, pp. 36–39.

——. *Involving Parents in Children's Learning, A Handbook for Teachers.* Pacific Oaks College, Whittier, California. Undated.

——. Project Head Start. *Parents Are Needed. Suggestion on Parent Participation in Child Development Centers*, No. 6. U.S. Department of Health, Education and Welfare, Washington, D.C. Undated.

Sources of Information about Infants and Children

8

After studying this chapter, you should be able to:

1. Outline the values and problems in using research reports on work with young children
2. Discuss the importance of description of *subjects,* size of *sample, measures* of behavior, *research setting,* and *statistical analysis* in evaluating child development research
3. Analyze the applicability of findings of a study to a particular group of children
4. List sources of information about infants and children available to the professional worker
5. Outline a method of observing children objectively
6. Describe the use of *observation records* in working with parents, students in training, and volunteers in a day care center

Professional workers differ from other workers in the responsibility they take in searching for ways to become more effective in their work with children. This chapter examines several ways to gain new information that may be applied to work with young children. The first way is probably the most difficult for beginners—reading research reports.

Value of Research

You may ask why getting information from research reports is necessary for people who work from day to day with young children. Why can't we learn what we need to know about children from other workers who have had years of experience?

You will learn a great deal from other workers, but techniques you learn from them may not be always in the best interest of young children. Long experience working with children sometimes results in more concern for the welfare of the adults than for that of the children. Sending children to sit in their lockers when they have deliberately knocked over someone's block building helps the adult by removing the problem behavior, but this guidance does little to help the children work out their problems with each other.

Some of you will ask, why not use "common sense"? Checking with your friends, you may find that "common sense" varies from individual to individual. In fact, "common sense" could be defined as each person's well-worn prejudices. "Common sense" for each individual is made up of attitudes and values established through one's unique experience in a family, as well as in school, through friends, and through other sources of influence such as TV, movies, and the printed word in newspapers, magazines, and books. Depending on "common sense" alone may make us too concerned about certain childish behavior. For example, our society places great emphasis on property rights. Without an understanding of the length of time required for children to gain an understanding of "mine" and "yours," you may label as stealing children's taking home in their pockets pieces of equipment from the center.

Memories of our own experiences in school influence our thinking about children. School experiences, as well as living in a culture that values work, affects our thinking about the value of play. We tend to expect children to enter public schools similar to the ones we remember. As a result, we may feel more comfortable when children are in an activity like memorizing numbers than when they are involved in play of their own choosing. We forget that schools, like other institutions, are changing. Many kindergarten and first grade teachers are giving children an opportunity to move around the classrooms, talk with other children, and work on individual or group projects of their own choosing, instead of requiring them to sit and listen quietly.

Problems in Applying Research Findings

As was pointed out in Chapter 1, our knowledge of how children grow and learn is based on studies of groups of children, but there are always exceptions, who do not fit with findings based on groups. This means that we have to be ready to accept the fact that certain children may not show reactions we might expect from our reading of research reports.

Another problem is the time and skill required to read research reports. Child development research is reported through many avenues, from the news media to the professional journals. It is tempting to accept reports one hears through the news media, because they are easier to understand. You may be discouraged when you first glance at a research report because of the new confusing words, numbers, and symbols. When you can accept the fact that you can learn from the report without understanding every word and every number, you have made a significant step in your ability to read research.

Beginners are also discouraged by the fact that studies of the same question report different findings. For example, there are a number of studies in the literature concerning the effect on IQ of nursery school attendance. Several studies report gains, and others report no change. One reason for this could be the variation one might expect in giving an IQ test to preschool children, as discussed in Chapter 5. Larger gains were evident in children (such as children in an orphanage) who had been receiving little attention and stimulation prior to planned group experience.[1] Therefore, another explanation for conflicting results in these studies is that earlier experiences of the subjects under study differ widely.

Similar findings from more than one study should serve as a basis for large changes in a center program. These findings should also fit with existing knowledge of children. One area of research that attracted considerable attention concerned teaching preschool children to read with the use of a "talking typewriter"—a typewriter programmed to permit hitting letters in their proper sequence for a specific spoken word. The research showed that it was possible to teach young children to associate words with certain groups of letters, in other words to learn to read. However, there has been no evidence that reading at age three or four influences later success in school or that the words associated with the letters necessarily had any meaning for young children. Fortunately, the "talking typewriter" was too expensive to encourage widespread use. Professionals who had observed children, knew how to evaluate research, and were aware of past reports of teaching reading to preschoolers would have been skeptical until they had examined the research reports. We will now examine some of the techniques and problems in carrying on research, so that you can better evaluate reports of studies that could influence the way you work with children.

Evaluating Research

THE HYPOTHESIS OR RESEARCH QUESTION

The opening paragraph of a research report outlines what the researcher hoped to learn from the study. Researchers may formulate a *hypothesis* or *research question,* a best guess for what they may find based on previous research. If the findings of the study agree with the hypothesis, the researchers accept the hypothesis; if the findings disagree with the hypothesis, they reject it. Frequently, researchers outline a question or questions they hope to answer without formulating a specific hypothesis.

As a beginning in reading research, you may find it helpful to read far enough into the report to discover the hypothesis or questions to be answered and then read the summary and conclusions to learn what was found. In some reports, this information is outlined for you in the abstract at the beginning. Having this information helps in evaluating the total study.

SUBJECTS

A description of the *subjects* (children, parents, teachers) usually follows the introduction. The number and description of the subjects is important. Because of the wide variation in human beings, the more children studied, the greater confidence researchers have in their findings. Finding a *sample* (the group of subjects selected for study) of infants or preschool children is more difficult than finding a sample of school-age children, since no institution like the public schools brings together most infants and preschool children in groups. Usually twenty or more subjects are preferable.

Selection of subjects is as important as number. You

need to know how similar the subjects of the study are to the children in your day care center. Consider the age, sex, and race of children, and the socioeconomic level of the family (usually measured by income and education of parents). Within the sample, the subjects should be as much alike as possible.

For example, to study the influence of spanking on the amount of physical aggression (hitting, pinching, biting) shown by children in a day care center, researchers might select children and parents who are as alike as possible in all respects except for parental use of spanking. They would select boys or girls of the same age, or, if they study both sexes, they would look at the results separately for boys and girls because there is evidence that the amount of physical aggression differs according to sex. The more the children and families are alike, the more confident the researchers can be that any relationship they find between spanking and physical aggression in the day care center will hold for other similar children and families.

While some studies look at the relationship between two variables, such as the relationship between spanking in the home and the children's physical aggression in a group situation, other studies divide the subjects into two groups, an *experimental* and a *control group*. These experimental studies examine the effect of a certain experience of treatment on a group of children. The experimental group would receive the treatment and the control group would not receive the treatment.

For example, researchers might be interested in examining the effect of a particular method of recording children's stories on tape, to help black children learn standard English. The best design for such a study would be to locate a group of black children and randomly assign them to an experimental or a control group by some such method as flipping a coin. This method would give each subject the opportunity to fall into either group. Frequently, this *randomized grouping* is not possible. Next the researchers locate groups of black children with whom they try out tape recordings of stories and in an effort to find a group of children as much alike as possible, to serve as a control group. In any study using an experimental group, the researcher should plan some special attention for the control group unrelated to the research question, in order to show that any change that occurred was due to the use of taped stories and not to the special attention the children received at the time their stories were taped.

MEASURES

Whether or not researchers' findings will be repeated in future studies depends to some extent on the *measures* they select. Measurement of human behavior is difficult. Even the relatively simple task of determining how frequently parents spank their children presents a variety of problems. First, there is the question of whether parents can remember how often they spank particular children in a given day, week, or month. (There is evidence that parents have difficulty remembering even more objective information, such as the age at which children began to walk.) Then there is the question of whether parents are willing to report their perceptions of their own behavior to researchers, either on a questionnaire or in an interview. Uncertain parents who have read that spanking is an undesirable method of child control may be more apt to change what they think they do when they report to the researchers than the more experienced or self-confident parents. Observation in the home or videotaped recordings of parent behavior may give more precise information as to how differently parents may behave when they are aware they are being observed.

RESEARCH SETTING

The situation in which behavior is studied is called the *research setting*. There are two types of research settings—naturalistic and experimental. An example of a naturalistic setting would be the day care center or the home. An experimental setting might be a room with specialized equipment, such as materials to draw responses from the children and, perhaps, an observation window and recording devices such as audiotapes or videotapes. Factors that may influence results can be more easily controlled in an experimental setting, but results obtained in an experimental setting may not always be applicable in a home or day care center. Behavior modification research has shown that changes in behavior in one situation, such as the school, do not automatically produce changes in behavior in another situation, such as the home.[2]

STATISTICAL ANALYSIS

Since researchers can study only a small sample from the population, they must use *statistical analysis* to determine how frequently the findings for a particular sample might be expected on the basis of chance alone. Until you have had a course in statistics, you will have to accept researchers' conclusions about the statistical significance of their findings. Editorial boards of research journals check the statistical analysis of each report, so you are not entirely dependent on the researchers' judgment.

EVALUATIVE QUESTIONS

Here are some questions to focus your thinking as you read a study. These questions will be most helpful if you try them out on one of the studies listed at the end of this chapter.

1. What was the researcher's question or hypothesis? Is this topic important to you in your work with your group of children?
2. How many and what kind of children or families

were studied? You will naturally have more confidence in a study of twenty or more subjects than in a study of ten or fewer subjects.

3. What flaws can you see in the measure? For example, did the researchers observe children or did they ask busy teachers to rate children?
4. Was the research setting similar to the one where you are working? If the researchers observed children in a day care center instead of observing one child at a time in a small room especially designed for observation of children, you can be more confident that the results apply to the setting where you teach. Also, if observing in two centers, one with toy guns and one without, were the centers similar in program and staff except for availability of guns?
5. Were the findings analyzed statistically? Did the statistical analysis yield significant results? For example, you will be more confident that it is worth the effort to remove guns from the day care center and ask children not to bring them from home if the relationship between the availability of guns and hitting of the toy clown is statistically significant.
6. What were the researchers' conclusions? If the hypothesis was accepted, you will be interested in what the researchers think the findings mean to workers with young children. If no relationship was found between the availability of toy guns and physical aggression, for instance, you will be interested in whether the researchers consider the hypothesis unsound or whether they see other reasons for its lack of support in this particular study.

Benefiting from Research

PROFESSIONAL JOURNALS

You will find research reports and summaries of research in two types of professional journals. The first type is the journal that is devoted entirely to research on children and their families—*Child Development* and *Developmental Psychology* are examples. Such publications often are available in libraries, and browsing through them can be informative. Usually the first page of each study carries an *abstract,* a brief summary of the most important information in that report; sample subjects and measures used (details usually omitted in magazine and newspaper reports) are included.

The second type of journal is that written specifically for teachers of young children. *Young Children,* published by the National Association for the Education of Young Children, and *Childhood Education,* from the Association for Childhood Education International, are examples. When you have adequate income, you will want to belong to one of these two organizations, and as a member you will receive the journal. Until you can afford to belong, you may be able to borrow copies from a member of the staff at your center.

In addition to very practical information on topics such as cooking experiences for children, these journals for teachers include occasional research reports and, more frequently, summaries of research reports, such as a summary of studies on language development influences. These summaries provide one person's interpretation of a group of research findings. Bibliographies given at the ends of these summary reports may include useful references to other studies. Summaries vary in quality. You will want to examine the date of publication of the research reports and the journals that published them as well as the qualifications of the person writing the summary.

PROFESSIONAL BOOKS

Another resource for day care workers is a library of books on child development, day care, and preschool education. Books provide summaries of findings on particular subjects, such as dependent behavior. Unfortunately, books are expensive and quickly become out-dated. In a large center, you will be able to share books with other staff members.

Before you consider buying a book, note the publication date and the author's qualifications. Select authors who have had professional experience that leads you to think they know the particular field. Parents and teachers who write about their experiences with children contribute to our understanding, but you must remember that teachers and parents have had experience with a limited number of children and usually have not thoroughly examined the research literature. For a book that has been revised, note the dates of the references in the bibliography. Some books are revised without extensive change in content and thus may not reflect the current thinking in the field.

PROFESSIONAL ORGANIZATIONS

Reading is not the only avenue open to help you grow in your professional field. Conferences sponsored by professional organizations provide one of the most enjoyable means of gaining information and developing your own ideas about programs for young children. In addition to stimulation provided by speakers and workshop leaders, you have the opportunity to compare your ideas and experiences with others in similar positions working with young children. Some organizations provide newsletters that give information about conferences and pending legislation affecting programs for young children.

Speakers at professional meetings vary in the extent that their statements are based on published information about children. Some speakers may attempt to hold the audience's interest by exaggerating statements for shock effect. You need to evaluate what you hear. You can discuss any ideas that do not fit in with your own experience with other professionals you meet at the conference.

Comparing your ideas about children with other workers is an important learning experience, but there are hazards. Such discussions can be a sharing of ignorance. As indicated before, techniques that may make adults' work easier may not always contribute to the children's well-being. Before you change your opinions after a discussion with others, look for evidence in research, professional journals, or books.

IN-SERVICE TRAINING AND WORKSHOPS

Although public school personnel have had released time for in-service meetings with supervisors and other teachers, workers in day care centers have had little opportunity for in-service training. This situation is changing. As centers increase in size and use volunteers more frequently, several staff members at once can be given released time to attend special workshops given by professionals in the community or to work with a supervisor on a portion of the program that needs improvement. This type of in-service training can be invaluable as a means of gaining both new information and new perspectives on your work. Workshops can be boring, however, if you make little effort to participate or share in the decisions relating to topics you discuss. Even more important is your willingness to try out your new ideas when working with the children.

With all the knowledge you gain from reading, professional meetings, and in-service training, you can approach the observation of children, another important way of learning, from a better informed position.

Observation of Infants and Children

Day care workers' thoughtful observation of children in their groups on each working day in the center provides an opportunity to learn more about children in general and especially about particular children.

Making *objective observation records* for individual children's behavior stimulates you to observe more carefully. Behavior records help you to be more objective, since without them you tend to remember certain children and behaviors more clearly than others. Because you will forget details of an incident as you cope with the pressures of working with children, you should record behavior when it happens or as soon after as possible. When recording at the time is not possible, jot down some records as you remember them, when children are resting quietly at naptime or at the end of the day.

There is a variety of ways to make behavior records. Recording significant behaviors on a note pad is one useful method. These records can be kept in the children's files along with health records and other information. Here is an example.

Name of Child ———— Date ———— Place ———— By (Initials of Observer)

John was putting pieces in a puzzle, looking only at the puzzle. Billy was taking long blocks from the shelf and piling them on the floor about three feet from John. Suddenly John pushed back his chair, jumped up, and ran toward Billy, vigorously kicking over Billy's pile of blocks. John ran back to the table, sat down in the same chair, picked up remaining piece of puzzle, put it in, held up the puzzle to show me, saying, "Look what I did!" as I walked toward him.

Note that this record describes only the observed behavior.

Two common errors are likely when you begin to make behavior records. One is to give a possible reason for the behavior along with the description of the behavior. In the example above, you might have written, "John was angry with Billy so he kicked over Billy's pile of blocks." John *may* have been angry over something Billy did to him earlier in the day. He *may* have wanted

Billy to let him join in block building. John *may* have been bored working his puzzle and knocked down Billy's pile of blocks to see what would happen.

You really cannot decide what caused John to knock over the blocks until you have thought about your past experiences with John and about what happened earlier that day. You would be better able to make guesses about the cause or causes if you record what immediately preceded the incident as well as a description of his posture and facial expression while he knocked over the blocks, as well as Billy's response.

A second error is to label a child. For example, you might add to the observation record about John, "John is an aggressive child." These labels reflect our own biases and may influence us to continue those biases in future observing. You may label as "aggressive" what other professionals consider expected behavior for John at his particular age in that particular situation. Having attached "aggressive" to John, you may look for hurting behavior in John and not see positive kinds of behavior like sympathy. Another reason to avoid labels is that John's behavior, like that of other children, changes from minute to minute. No label is ever adequate to describe a child.

As you review records you have made on children, note the variety of behaviors you are recording. The biases we have developed as children, and possibly later as parents, influence our observations as well as our work with children. Compare behaviors you have recorded for a particular child with observations another worker has made on the same child to determine how each of you sees that child. We often see certain kinds of behavior and ignore other behavior in observation records, depending on the specific kinds of behavior that concern us.

All the children's files should be reviewed every month or as often as possible to evaluate their progress and to note whether some recent behavior records have been added. Some quiet children are often overlooked by the staff and behavior records are not made for them without such monthly reminders.

Observation records have many uses in the center's program. They can be helpful in:

1. understanding particular children, such as those who disrupt the program through hurting other children
2. planning the daily program in the center around the interests and abilities of the children
3. helping volunteers and parents who may volunteer to assist in the program to understand particular children
4. specific examples of behavior to help parents understand statements you make about their children in conferences

In summary, workers with children have several avenues for learning about children in general—reading, professional meetings, in-service training. Workers also have the opportunity each working day to learn more about infants and children in their care. The workers' success with these infants and children will be influenced by the use they make of these opportunities.

Glossary

Abstract Brief summary of the most important information in a report.

Control group Research subjects not receiving specialized treatment under study.

Experimental group Research subjects designated to receive a particular treatment under study.

Measure The method used for evaluating behavior under study.

Objective observation record Descriptive records of behavior that do not include the observers' own feelings or interpretations.

Randomized grouping   Organization of research so that all subjects in the sample have equal opportunity to fall into either the experimental or the control group. Flipping a coin can help you divide subjects randomly.

Research question or *hypothesis*   A best guess based on observation or research evidence, to be accepted or rejected on the basis of information gathered in a particular study.

Research setting   A situation in which behavior is studied and evaluated. The settings chosen can be naturalistic or experimental.

Sample   The group of subjects selected for study from the total population.

Statistical analysis   The techniques for numerical analysis to determine how frequently findings of a study can be expected on the basis of chance alone.

Subjects   The specific children or adults selected for study.

Study Questions

1. Ask a worker in an infant or preschool center to select for you two infants or preschool children he or she would like you to observe, or if this is not possible select two infants or children who appear interesting to you. Observe the two children for a period of at least an hour. Following the suggestions in this chapter, record at least four incidents of behavior you consider significant. If possible discuss these behaviors with a fellow student or an adult working with these children.

2. With another person, observe a child, each of you recording behavior independently. After fifteen minutes compare your records. Note similarities and differences. Try to explain the reasons for your differences.

3. Read one of the following studies and describe the research question or hypothesis, number and kind of subjects, measures of behavior, research setting, researcher's evaluation of statistical significance, and researcher's evaluation of the results. Of what significance are the findings to a worker in day care?

> Brooks, Jeanne, and Lewis Michael. "Attachment Behavior in Thirteen-Month-Old, Opposite-Sex Twins." *Child Development* 45, 1974, pp. 243–247.
> Strommen, Ellen A. "Verbal Self-Regulation in a Children's Game: Impulsive Errors on 'Simon Says'." *Child Development* 44, 1973, pp. 849–853.
> Langlois, J., Nathan Gottfried, and B. Seay. "The Influence of Sex of Peer on the Social Behavior of Preschool Children." *Developmental Psychology* 8, 1973, pp. 93–98.

Notes

1. H. C. Dawe, "A Study of the Effect of an Educational Program upon Language Development and Related Mental Functions in Young Children," *Journal of Experimental Education,* 11, 1942, p. 207.
2. Robert G. Wahler, "Setting Generality: Some Specific and General Effects of Child Behavior Therapy," *Journal of Applied Behavior Analysis,* 2, 1969, p. 246.

Supplementary Readings

Almy, M. *The Early Childhood Educator at Work.* McGraw-Hill, New York, 1975.
Cohen, D., and V. Stern. *Observing and Recording the Behavior of Young Children.* Teachers College Press, New York, 1958.

Day Care in the United States— Past, Present, Future

9

After studying this chapter, you should be able to:

1. describe the most important programs for infants and young children during the past one hundred years
2. discuss the contributions and limitations of licensing in promoting quality day care programs
3. outline the advantages and disadvantages of day care homes as compared with day care centers
4. outline evidence of need for increased facilities for day care
5. explain the differences between custodial and comprehensive day care and possible effects of each on infants and children
6. discuss several unsolved problems in the field of day care
7. discuss values of importance to the professional day care worker

207

Present knowledge in any field is influenced by what has been learned from programs carried on in the past. In order to see your day-to-day work in perspective, you need some knowledge about past programs and ideas about children. This knowledge can serve as a base when you consider both problems now facing the field and trends for the future.

The Beginnings of Day Care

In this country's early days, orphaned children were assigned to almshouses—institutions that cared for the aged, handicapped, and insane. Placing children in such an institution reflected the belief that food, shelter, and clothing met all the needs of young children. Fortunately, many children were cared for by relatives, often to the advantage of all involved, since even young children were helpful in homes and on farms that depended on manual labor.

ORPHANAGES

The establishment of *orphanages* in the nineteenth century was considered a forward step, since orphanages were concerned only with children. A total of 1075 or-

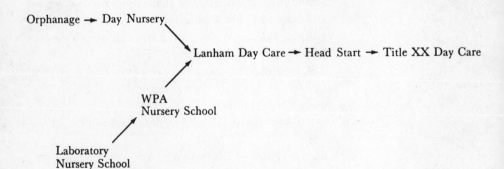

phanages and children's homes with a total of 92,887 residents existed in 1904, according to a publication of the Bureau of the Census (1905).[1]

In time, findings from research showed that young children needed meaningful relationships with one or two adults, and orphanages were then found to be undesirable. Care of infants and children for pay in *foster homes* or *day nurseries* (the earliest day care centers) replaced orphanage care for some children during the late nineteenth and early twentieth centuries. Some orphanages now exist but they care for relatively few infants and young children. Orphanages best serve the needs of older children who may be unable to adjust to foster homes.

DAY NURSERIES

Growth of day nurseries, caring for children eight to ten hours a day, influenced the decline of orphanages. The first day nursery was established in Boston in 1838 for children of seamen's wives and widows.[2] Toward the end of the century, an increasing number of day nurseries were established for infants and children of working mothers who had no outside source of support. One reason for this increase was the evidence for a relationship between maternal employment and infant mortality. Therefore, registered nurses were usually included on the staff of day nurseries. In most day nurseries, as compared with today's day care centers, more emphasis was placed on physical well-being than on emotional and intellectual development.

Compared to the number of day care centers at the present time, day nurseries were relatively few in number, and they were clustered in a few states. In 1904, according to the census report, there were 166 day nurseries in the United States, with an enrollment of 7441 infants and children. Of these, 113 were in four states—Massachusetts, New Jersey, New York, and Pennsylvania.

Several factors influenced the decline of the day nursery after 1910. The Mothers' Pension act of 1911 provided pensions for mothers of young children with no source of support. By 1918, public assistance was available to mothers in thirty-nine states. Findings from child development research raised questions about children's being separated from their mothers for long periods of time. During the 1930s, the federal government developed programs for young children that competed with the day nurseries. Therefore, let us look first at the influence of research programs on institutions caring for young children.

Growth of Child Development Research

The number of young men rejected for service in World War I because of physical and intellectual handicaps aroused concern that led to a search for the relationship of physical and mental deficits in adults to care in early childhood. Research on development of preschool children increased rapidly between 1920 and 1930, and the laboratory nursery school was an important outgrowth of this research interest. Laboratory nursery schools were established in colleges and universities to provide groups of young children for study.

Nursery schools established for poor children in England, as well as the day nursery in the United States, influenced the laboratory nursery schools. Unlike the day nurseries and nursery schools, however, the laboratory schools enrolled middle-class children. Middle-class families could transport children to school, supply necessary information about the children's past and present experiences, and pay tuition to supplement nursery school budgets.

The laboratory nursery school program covered a period similar to that of the public school day—about

9:00 A.M. to 3:00 P.M. Unlike many day nurseries of that period, these programs supplied materials, like blocks, that are now considered basic to a good program. Generally, the educational philosophy was to let children explore these materials on their own as long as they obeyed the rules established by the center staff. Extensive records were kept on children's eating, sleeping, and eliminating habits.

Federal Programs for Young Children

Information gained through laboratory schools' recorded observations supplied data for extensive reports given at the White House Conference on Children in 1930. Although the first White House Conference was held in 1909, the federal government did not become involved in programs for groups of preschool children until after 1930.

WPA NURSERY SCHOOLS

The Works Progress Administration (WPA), established to combat adverse conditions of the Depression, included nursery schools as part of its program. The expressed purpose of the *WPA nursery schools* was to provide employment for unemployed teachers, social workers, nurses, and nutritionists. The program, staff, equipment, and length of program day were all similar to those of the laboratory nursery schools. Like *Head Start* of the 1960s, WPA nursery schools served only poor children. However, a greater variety of social backgrounds was represented because at that time all types of families were poor.

An important contribution of the WPA nursery schools was the increased public awareness of the possible value of group programs for young children.

Another was stimulation of further research and writing on such programs. Public interest and related publications had a positive effect on the day nurseries still in existence at that time.

LANHAM DAY CARE CENTERS

Some WPA nursery schools were still operating when money was made available for day care centers under the Lanham Act. With entry of the United States into World War II, women gained many opportunities to work outside the home. According to the Lanham Act, federal funds could be made available to local communities for day care of children when women were needed to replace men in war-related employment.

Lanham day care centers were both similar and different from the WPA nursery schools. Most Lanham centers were open for twelve hours, and some were open for eighteen hours. The basic materials and activities offered the children were similar, with modifications made necessary by the longer day. The longer day also required a staggered staffing pattern, with some workers opening the center and others staffing late in the day, with some midday overlap. These day care centers were the first programs to employ large numbers of teachers trained in child development. Nurses and nutritionists were involved, at least on a consultant basis, but no social casework service was available.

The program in the Lanham centers also differed somewhat from that of day nurseries and WPA nursery schools. More concern was shown for the children's emotional and intellectual development and slightly less attention was given to physical well-being. In effect, these centers gave more attention to the "whole" child.

The Lanham centers introduced the term "day care" to describe all day programs for young children, and because the Lanham day care centers served children from all types of families, these centers also made the general public aware that day care could be an important resource for middle-class as well as low-income families.

Within six months after the end of World War II, federal funds were withdrawn from the Lanham centers. Some were able to continue with the combined support of tuition and state or local funds. Since quality day care is expensive, the quality of these programs, as compared with the earlier Lanham centers program, generally deteriorated.

Recent Developments

HEAD START

Head Start was started because of concern for children, rather than because of employment or convenience of adults. It began in 1965 as a summer program for poor children, in order to improve their chances for later success in school. In most communities, this beginning evolved into a year-round program, varying the day's length according to the needs of community families.

Head Start made two important contributions to day care program standards. The first is its comprehensive nature. Head Start has further developed the concept of working with the "whole" child through a program that includes medical, dental, and social services.

The second contribution has been the concept of parent *involvement* rather than parent *education*. Parent involvement emphasizes contribution and decision-making, rather than simply education as to what the center staff considers appropriate parental behavior.

Head Start has been criticized. One reason for the criticism may be the unrealistic expectations the general public, including Congress, has held for Head Start. One extensive study with some obvious limitations showed that summer Head Start programs had little effect on children's later success in school and full-year programs were only marginally effective.[3] Obviously, no one program can erase such influences of poverty as poor nutrition and lack of a stimulating learning environment for four or five years prior to enrollment in Head Start. However, people who have worked with Head Start can describe many examples of families that regained hope and self-respect through participation. Employment of mothers of Head Start children in programs has enabled some mothers to become professional workers with young children. Acting as volunteers in the daily program with children, many parents, especially mothers, have learned a variety of techniques for working with their children. Undoubtedly what parents learned in Head Start affected all the children in the family, but this side effect is difficult to measure.

TITLE IV-A DAY CARE CENTERS

Title IV-A, a 1962 amendment to the Social Security Act, permitted inclusion of day care as a social service through state departments of welfare. Since this provision of the Social Security Act required matching funds from local communities, growth of these centers has been uneven over the country. Like Head Start, these centers have been limited to serving poor children. A number of *Title IV-A day care programs* also have been comprehensive, including medical as well as social services for families. In some communities, parents have been included on boards making decisions about center programs. This model of concern for the "whole" child in day care may influence future federal day care legislation. Title XX, which has now replaced Title IV-A, makes day care available to children from families representing a wider range of income levels.

Licensing of Day Care Centers

State governments have taken much of the responsibility, through day care licensing, for protection of children in group care programs. Although since the Civil War there has been some attempt to protect children receiving care outside the home, licensing has become an important influence on day care only since World War II. Legally, licensing involves passage of a law that states that certain kinds of programs for young children cannot exist unless the programs meet certain standards. A licensing law delegates to an agency the responsibility for establishing a set of requirements, and this agency issues licenses to programs that meet these requirements.

The state Departments of Public Welfare, with assistance from state Departments of Health and Education, are often responsible for licensing. However, a few states have delegated primary responsibility for licensing to the state Departments of Health or state Departments of Education.

Many licensing laws have been passed or revised during the past fifteen years, and laws and standards for the programs are constantly changing. At any one time it is difficult to describe licensing in all fifty states. According to a survey published in 1971, all fifty states had some kind of regulation of day care programs and most, but not all, required licensing of day care centers.[4]

The purpose of day care licensing is to set and enforce standards to protect children from physical and psychological hazards.[5] Standards for day care centers include requirements for building, including the amount of space for each child indoors and out, equipment, number and training of staff, and program for children, including nutrition. Unfortunately, it has been easier to evaluate plumbing and other safety features than to evaluate the quality of the program provided by the staff.

One role of the licensing agency is not to close centers, but to work with day care operators and assist them in meeting requirements.[6] From the authors' point of view, the work of the licensing workers in interpreting the basis for requirements has been an important influence in improving the quality of children's day care.

Family Day Care Homes

Standards for licensing day care in the period following World War II influenced the growth of *family day care homes.* Many states did not then permit children under age two in group day care. As indicated earlier in this chapter, observations of children in orphanages in group care situations during the war raised questions about the desirability of group care of infants. It appeared at that time that a day care situation where the infants could develop relationships with one adult seemed superior to group care. If care was not available in the infant's own home, care in another home that met certain standards seemed the best substitute.

The definition of a family day care home varies from state to state, but usually family day care home mothers are permitted to care for up to five to ten children, in addition to their own. The number of children under one year of age permitted to any one home usually is limited, however, to two.

According to one 1972 survey, there were 60,967 licensed or approved family day care homes, with capacity to care for 215,841 children, as compared with 20,319 licensed or approved day care centers with space to care for 805,361 children.[7] According to one estimate, however, fewer than 5 percent of the homes caring for children are licensed or supervised.[8] This estimate may be low, but many parents make informal arrangements for care of their children by neighbors or strangers.

The family day care home has advantages and disadvantages when compared with the day care center. The life style of the home may be more similar to that of children's families than the more institutionalized center. The family day care home is often more flexible in the hours care can be provided. Frequently the day care home is closer to children's own homes and fewer transportation problems arise. Care with relatives or friends may be easier for parents to arrange than group care. This type of care, however, may be second choice for many families. Willner found that 80 percent of the mothers questioned said they would switch to group care if it were available. Many of the mothers who said they would switch to group care gave as their reason that they felt group care was more reliable.[9]

One problem that probably appears more frequently with family as compared with center day care is the discontinuity in day care arrangements. According to the Willner study, around 25 percent of children under three and 34 percent of those between three and six have experienced four or more changes in day care arrangements. Probably many of these changes resulted from changing life situations for adults, like mothers moving and stopping work and day care mothers discontinuing care. Some of these changes would have occurred if the children were in center care, but since the family day care home is primarily dependent on one person, it seems logical that there would be more discontinuity in family day care.

Questions have been raised about the kind and variety of activities provided for children in family day care. F. A. Ruderman found that standards for family day care pay little attention to the quality of the day's activities. Family day care homes examined in her study received especially low ratings on developmental activities.[10]

There is a growing body of research indicating that infants do not suffer and may benefit from experiences in carefully planned group or center programs.[11] A combination of center and family day care homes to meet the needs of different types of infants and young children seems desirable. This has been demonstrated in at least one project.[12]

Continuing Needs

Helping family day care home mothers to improve the quality of the programs they provide for children is only one of the problems facing the day care field. It is evident that many children are in day care situations that are far from desirable.[13] More quality day care programs, at costs that middle- and low-income families can afford, are needed.

Let us look at some of the facts. Although the birth rate is declining, the number of working mothers is increasing. In comparing census information with a survey made in 1972, there were 1.5 million fewer children in families, but 650,000 more children had working mothers. Evidence for the need of these mothers to work outside the home can be found in the increase in families headed by women. Between 1970 and 1972, the number of children in two-parent families decreased by 1.8 million, and the number of children in families headed by women increased by 1.2 million. Many mothers who head families cannot pay the full cost of day care. The median income of the mother in families headed by women in 1972 was $5,795.[14]

Because of the rates of change in women's employment and in day care programs, it is impossible to estimate the lag between need and available day care at any one time. In March 1973, the number of children under six with working mothers was almost 6 million. The 1972 estimate of total licensed capacity for day care in homes and centers was slightly over a million.[15] Even though there is a year's difference between these estimates, it is obvious that licensed day care programs are not meeting the need.

The need is even greater for children with special handicaps. Few centers accept children with such special problems as blindness, hearing loss, or retardation. Some of these children could be integrated into a group of children who fall within the normal range of abilities, but more severely handicapped children need day care in a special group. Under either plan, day care programs for handicapped children are more expensive due to the need for more trained adults and special equipment.

In addition to more openings for infants and children in day care homes and day care centers, a variety of programs is needed. A child development approach to day care selects a program that is right for the children; it does not try to fit the children to the program. Some children seem to need a program that plans much of the day, while others seem to thrive on a program that includes large blocks of time for free play activities. Families should be able to choose a center with goals for children somewhat similar to their own. Children whose families value creativity should not be forced into a center that emphasizes following the rules. Some children fare better in groups of children of different ages; others learn and develop relations more readily in a group of children around their own ages. Some children and families need special help with medical and dental services as well as social work help with family problems, while others need only the day care program itself.

Unsolved Problems in Day Care

Unsolved problems vary according to location (urban or rural) climate, type of children and families, and relationships with the public schools the children enter when they leave the center. Only a few of the most important problems are discussed here.

PHYSICAL PLANT

Although discussion of buildings and playgrounds for groups of young children falls outside the realm of this book, we believe that the *physical plant* of the center or family day care home does influence the behavior of both children and adults. Many day care centers are located in buildings that were previously used for other purposes. Some renovated buildings have been developed into attractive, functional environments for children.[16] Other buildings have not been so fortunate!

Small, dark rooms and lack of sound-absorbent materials on ceilings, walls, and floor are problems in many converted centers. Young children at play should not be expected to be quiet, but high noise levels contribute to the fatigue of children and adults. Some children need an opportunity to get away from the group at times. Architects and day care workers should be able to design centers that would solve these problems.

Playgrounds for young children are often less attractive than the buildings. Too frequently, these playgrounds are asphalt rectangles with a few swings, a slide, and a jungle gym. Playgrounds in Europe and those recently proposed in this country contrast with those the authors have seen in many centers.[17] Workers in day care have a responsibility to convince boards and administrators that playgrounds should receive as much attention as buildings.

PLANNING FOR EACH CHILD

In programming, the important problem is planning for *individual* children. This planning must be done with the children's families. Techniques for communicating and developing a relationship with parents were discussed in Chapter 7.

Some of the fatigue and confusion infants and young children in centers are subject to is probably due to experiencing two very different worlds. Obviously, all differences between the center and the home cannot be eliminated. Children have to learn to live with a variety of adults and standards.

Workers should remember, however, that different children come from different backgrounds and different familial patterns. Some adults feel that all children in a group should be held to the same standards, for example, in eating behavior. Expecting children to eat neatly when they have not observed this kind of eating at home makes different demands on these children from those made on the children who have eaten with traditional middle-class families since infancy. Possibly because of their egocentricism, young children are not usually concerned about different requirements for different children. And, these years are a good time to begin learning to accept individual differences.

A day care program should not be considered preparation for the public schools. From a child development point of view, the best preparation for kindergarten or first grade is the best possible program for children at *their particular levels of development.*

As long as success in public school is important for success in the world, planning for children should consider the challenges they are likely to meet immediately after they leave the center. One experimental day care program, with enrollment beginning as early as the first year of life, is part of a public school, and the day care director serves as the school principal.[18] Whether the public schools can or should take the responsibility for day care of infants and young children is a question to be decided in the future. The need for better communication between day care workers and public school personnel is obvious.

Another question for the future is whether or not *custodial day care* is acceptable if funds are not available for a more comprehensive program. Custodial day care is concerned with children's physical safety while they are in the center. Such a program ignores the need for an education component. A truly *comprehensive day care* program is concerned with the development of the "whole" child, and includes medical and dental services and social services for the family. Some families can provide for medical and dental services for their children, but only the center can provide for the children's education at the center. Both casual observation and child development research supply evidence that children are learning all the time. Day care center staff need to be aware of what children are learning and make the best use of the children's time to promote their total development.

You, as a professional worker in day care, can play a part in eliminating custodial day care. Help all the people you know to understand the need to provide a day care program based on what is known about the development of children even though the more comprehensive programs cost more than custodial care. Considering the long-term effect of experiences in the early years, child development programs should be a promising investment in the coming generation.

Questions for Research

Ways to ease the transition between the day care center and the public schools is only one of the many unanswered questions relating to day care. Some of these questions must be answered by researchers. Little research has been done within the day care setting, and relatively few researchers have studied children who spend more than six hours a day away from home.

Workers in day care centers can help researchers by raising questions based on their own observations and by adapting their programs to research needs when necessary. Adults in the center are also responsible for protecting the children in their care from any adult, however, including researchers who make unrealistic demands.

Most children are pleased with the novelty of leaving the playroom with researchers if the researchers have taken time to get acquainted with them. Researchers with little experience with young children need to be reminded of the importance of gaining children's trust before involving them in a research project. Children should never be forced to go with researchers or forced to carry on tasks that are obviously uncomfortable for them.

Here are some questions that need to be researched. You will think of others.

1. What are the long-term effects of day care on children's relationship with their parents?
2. Does the age of admission to a day care program in infancy influence infants' attachment to mothers and other family members?
3. What size group and what kind of learning experiences are most appropriate for each age level?
4. Does the number of adults who interact with infants and toddlers affect behavior of most children? This is significant in planning for use of volunteers.
5. How does range of ages influence learning and the number of conflicts among children?

Day Care Worker as a Political Force

In the past, day care staff have been so involved in working with the children in their care that they have not been effective in influencing legislation relating to day care. Many children who need day care live in families who cannot meet the cost. Even middle- and upper-income families can seldom meet the full cost of day care at the time in their lives when they have young children. Funds to supplement what parents can afford to pay must come either through donations from people who believe in day care or from local, state, or federal government.

The public schools are subsidized by tax money. It seems logical that part of the costs for day care also should be shared. Adequate financial support for day care will come only after a long period of education of the public, and especially of our political leaders. We all can discuss the needs and values of day care with our friends and neighbors. But that is not enough. We also must write and talk with political leaders at all levels of government. Through professional organizations, we can learn of pending legislation and write to appropriate leaders who will vote on that legislation.

In addition to influencing legislation for children, those committed to professional work with children have a responsibility to protect children's rights outside as well as in the center. Child abuse has been increasing. As a day care worker, you have an opportunity to see evidence of child abuse because you know the children and see them frequently. If a child has been hurt physically or deliberately frightened outside the center, you should discuss this with your director or social worker. You can work with the person who is responsible for reporting this type of information to your local welfare department.

Values of the Worker in Day Care

In serving as an advocate for children and in daily work with children, professional workers are influenced by their own personal values. Being aware of your values and being able to define these values for children and adults contributes to your satisfaction and effectiveness in your work.

First, you must be convinced that day care can be a good experience for children. Of course you cannot be expected to endorse all kinds of day care programs. You must be convinced that the day care you are providing is valuable for most children. If you find you have strong reservations about the appropriateness of a certain type of program, you would not be an effective worker in that program. We are not suggesting, naturally, blind loyalty to any program. No worker will be satisfied with all aspects of a program, but most workers should be satisfied with the experiences of most of the children in their care.

A second area of values revolves around your regard

for the importance of your behavior. Day care workers must have convictions about their ability to influence children. Throughout this book we have stressed the influence adults have on the children in their care. We have discussed the value of a warm personal relationship between adults and children during these critically important seventy-two months of life. There will be times when you feel you can do little to influence the behavior of a particular child, but your general outlook must be one of confidence. You must feel that you can and do make a difference in the lives of children. This attitude influences your whole approach to day care work.

A third and very important value relates to your confidence in the potential of human beings. This confidence influences your own growth as well as your capacity to guide children. In the past, our culture has held the Puritan belief that children are born in sin and are naturally sinful. Children generally live up to the expectations we have for them. To help each child reach his potential, we must be confident that, in a good environment, he or she will develop into a capable, responsible human being. This includes a good physical plant, adequate food, stimulating learning experiences, friends to love and be loved by in return and, above all, the freedom to be a child.

Children as they are today are human beings. They are born with the right to live life to its fullest. We must offer them no less. The authors feel that through a child development approach to day care we can provide children with an opportunity to develop their potential and recognize in others the rights and responsibilities of being human beings.

Glossary

Comprehensive day care   Programs concerned with all aspects of children's welfare, including physical well-being, mental development and their feelings about themselves and others as influenced by the center and the home.

Custodial day care   Provides physically safe environment with minimal attention to education and psychological safety.

Day care licensing   Regulation of day care centers by state governments to protect infants and children in day care from physical and psychological hazards.

Day nursery   Established in the 1800s to care for infants and young children of working mothers. Replaced by the day care center after World War II.

Family day care homes   Provide care for part of the day for limited number of infants and young children within a home setting.

Foster home   Provides twenty-four-hour care for one or several children in a home setting.

Head Start   A comprehensive program for young children in lower-income families established as part of the War on Poverty in 1965.

Lanham day care centers   Long day programs for young children established during World War II to enable mothers to work in war-related industry.

Orphanage   Provides twenty-four-hour care for homeless children, frequently in large groups.

Title IV-A day care programs   Comprehensive day care for lower-income children financed by local and federal funds under Title IV-A of the Social Security Act.

WPA nursery schools   The first federal program for education of children under the age of six; sponsored by the Works Progress Administration during the Depression.

Study Questions

1. Trace the trend in child care from emphasis on physical well-being to concern for the "whole" child, be-

ginning with orphanages and following through to Title IV-A day care.

2. What factors other than concern for children have influenced programs for group care of infants and young children?

3. Examine the licensing requirements for day care centers and family day care homes in your state. If possible, interview licensing workers to discuss their views on the contributions and problems of day care licensing.

4. Talk with parents of children in day care about their problems in making day care arrangements for their children.

5. Discuss with kindergarten or first grade teachers what skills they would like children to have on entering their programs.

6. Ask a local official to visit your class to discuss ways of influencing legislation for young children.

7. Ask a director of a day care center to talk about values he or she considers important for center staff members.

Notes

1. U.S. Bureau of Census, *Benevolent Institutions 1904*, Government Printing Office, Washington, D.C., 1905, p. 26.

2. V. Kerr, "Child Care's Long American History," in *Child Care—Who Cares?*, ed. P. Roby, New York, Basic Books, 1973, p. 158.

3. Westinghouse Learning Corporation, *The Impact of Head Start*, Office of Economic Opportunity, Washington, D.C., 1969, p. 8.

4. Office of Child Development, *State and Local Day Care Licensing Requirements*, DHEW Publication N(OCD)73–1066, Washington, D.C., p. 4.

5. G. Morgan, *Regulations of Early Childhood Programs*,

rev. ed., Day Care and Child Development Council of America, Washington, D.C., 1973, p. 34.

6. *Ibid,* p. 101.

7. *Voice for Children,* "New National Child Care Statistics," 7, No. 11 (1974), p. 3.

8. M. Keyserling, *Windows on Day Care,* National Council of Jewish Women, New York, 1972, p. 5.

9. M. Willner, "Family Day Care: An Escape from Poverty," *Social Work,* 16 (1971), pp. 32–33.

10. F. A. Ruderman, *Child Care and Working Mothers: A Study of Arrangements Made for Daytime Care of Children,* Child Welfare League of America, New York, 1968, p. 351.

11. B. Caldwell, "Can Young Children Have a Quality Life in Day Care?" in *Providing the Best for Young Children,* ed. J. McCarthy & C. May, National Association for the Education of Young Children, Washington, D.C., 1974, p. 25.

12. J. Sale, "Family Day Care—a Valuable Alternative," in *Providing the Best for Young Children,* ed. J. McCarthy & C. May, National Association for the Education of Young Children, Washington, D.C., 1974, pp. 31–33.

13. Keyserling, p. 1.

14. A. Young, "Children of Working Mothers," *Monthly Labor Review,* 96 (1973), p. 39.

15. *Voice for Children,* "New National Child Care Statistics," 7, No. 11 (1974), p. 3.

16. Educational Facilities Laboratories, *Found Spaces and Equipment for Children's Centers.* New York: Educational Facilities Laboratory, 1972, pp. 5–69.

17. A. Ledermann and A. Trachsel, *Creative Playgrounds and Recreation Centers,* 2nd ed., Frederick A. Praeger, New York, 1968; Southeastern Day Care Project, *Planning Playgrounds for Day Care,* Southern Regional Education Board, Atlanta, 1973.

18. S. Braun and E. Edwards, *History and Theory of Early Childhood Education,* Charles A. Jones, Worthington, Ohio, 1972, p. 373.

Supplementary Readings

Allen, S., et al. *Perspectives on Child Care.* National Association for the Education of Young Children, Washington, D.C., 1972.

Breitbart, V., ed. *The Day Care Book.* Alfred A. Knopf, New York, 1974.

Fein, F., and A. Clarke-Stewart. *Day Care in Context.* John Wiley, New York, 1973.

Kritchevsky, S., E. Prescott, and L. Walling. *Planning Environments for Young Children—Physical Space.* National Association for the Education of Young Children, Washington, D.C., 1969.

Glossary

Abstract   Brief summary of the most important information in a report.

Accommodation   In Piaget's theory, a concept describing changes in one's existing ideas or actions as a result of the process of assimilation.

Achievement   Children's attempt to win approval for competence, more frequently researched in relationship to academic learning.

Active vocabulary   Words understood and used in speech.

Aggression   Verbal (ridiculing) or physical (hitting) behavior directed toward injuring another person.

Articulation   Learning of speech sounds and the rules for using these sounds.

Assimilation   Concept from Piaget's theory describing individual's incorporating a new experience into ideas or actions already acquired.

Attachment   Tendency of the young to seek to be near chief caretaker and a few others.

Autonomy   Second stage in Erikson's theory of personality development covering second and third years of life. Child develops a sense of independence with ability to use help and guidance of others.

Babbling   Wide range of sounds produced by the infant, most frequently during the second half of the first year.

Behaviorism   Psychological theory that emphasizes learning.

Behavior modification   Technology outlining strategy for changing behavior.

Cephalocaudal trend   Directional trend of development noted in motor development. Development proceeds from head to lower part of body.

Classification   Categorizing objects or events around one or more dimensions, such as color or holidays.

Communication style   Unique way the individual uses language to express thoughts and feelings and to clarify ideas.

Comprehensive day care   Concerned with all aspects of child's welfare, including physical well-being, development of the mind, and feelings about the self and others as influenced by the center and the home.

Conservation problem   Test of the child's ability to recognize that a quantity remains the same when it changes shape or position.

Control group   Subjects not receiving specialized treatment under study.

Cooing   Limited variety of non-crying sounds produced by the infant, most frequently prior to the time the infant is able to sit up.

Cooperative play   Two or more children playing together.

Creativity   Willingness to engage in fantasy and in forming new hypotheses; ability to use knowledge in original and constructive ways.

Culture   Set of customs and learned behavior in a particular group of people.

Custodial day care   Provides physically safe environment with minimal attention to education and psychological safety.

Day care licensing   Regulation of day care centers by state governments to protect infants and children in day care.

Day nursery   Established in the 1800s to care for infants and young children of working mothers. Replaced by the day care center after World War II.

Dependence   Desire for help or attention from another individual.

Egocentricism   A thinking deficiency in all young children, who are concerned with self, looking at all things in relation to themselves.

Ethology   Science of animal behavior.

Experimental group   Subjects designated to receive a particular treatment.

Family day care homes   Provide care for part of the day for a limited number of infants and young children within a home setting.

Fine motor skills   Ability to coordinate small muscles of the hands.

Foster home   Provides twenty-four-hour care for one or several children in a home setting.

Frustration   A barrier that prevents the individual from getting what he wants. This barrier may be another individual, an object, or the individual's own lack of skill.

Generation of hypotheses   Formation of "best guesses" about solutions to a problem.

Gross motor skills   Ability to coordinate large muscles of the body.

Head Start   Comprehensive program for poor young children established as part of the War on Poverty in 1965.

Hypothesis   A best guess based on observation.

Infancy   Age range from birth to one year of age.

Initiative   Stage of Erikson's theory covering third through fifth year of life. Child develops ability to formulate plans and carry them out without much concern for his skills.

Kinesthetic sense   Individual's awareness of the position of the body in space.

Landmarks of development   Physical characteristics or behavior that may be expected of certain age levels but, because of individual differences in development, may not appear at the indicated times.

Lanham day care centers   Long-day programs for young children established during World War II to enable mothers to work in war-related industry.

Learning   Changes in behavior due to experience.

Maternal guilt   Mother's bad feelings toward herself for not living up to certain expectations.

Maturation Developmental changes appearing with increase in age and relatively independent of environmental factors.

Measure Method used for evaluating behavior under study.

Mobiles Hanging objects which move with air currents.

Modeling Learning a behavior by observing another's performance of that behavior.

Motor development Changing abilities in control of the body, such as walking, climbing, grasping, and handling objects.

Nesting toys Objects of graduated size that fit inside each other; very helpful in the development of fine motor skills.

Objective observation record Descriptive record of behavior that does not include the observer's feelings or interpretation of behavior.

Object or *person permance* Awareness that people and objects exist even when the infant cannot see them.

Onlooker play Watching and enjoying the play of others.

Ordinal position Determined by order of birth in the family.

Orphanage Provides twenty-four-hour care for children without families, frequently in large groups.

Parallel play Playing beside, although not actually with, another child.

Parent Advisory Council Representative group of parents, having power to advise the organization.

Parent education Staff and parents working together, trying to improve parenting techniques and increase parental knowledge.

Parent-initiated meeting Meeting held at the request of parents or organized entirely by parents.

Parent involvement Staff and parents working together, with parents directly or indirectly involved in all aspects of the program, including decision-making positions.

Passive vocabulary Words understood but not used in speech.

Physical environment   Space and materials available to the child in his or her surroundings.

Play yard   Equipment to keep infant in a specific area, frequently referred to as playpen.

Preoperational period   In Piaget's theory, the stage covering the period from two to six years of age. It differs from the preceding stage in that the children are able to use language in thinking.

Processing information   Attending to features in the environment, organizing, evaluating, and manipulating concepts from these impressions.

Proximodistal trend   Directional trend in development. Development proceeds from center to periphery of the body.

Psycholinguists   Those who study how the child uses the capacity to learn language in understanding and producing sounds and words.

Randomized grouping   All subjects in the sample have equal chance of falling into either the experimental or the control group.

Redirection   Suggesting or insisting on a change in behavior, usually in a situation where an adult is helping a child change from unacceptable to more acceptable behavior.

Reflex   Automatic response to a stimulus.

Reinforcement   Social or material reward for a particular behavior. Reinforcement increases the probability that the reinforced behavior will occur again.

Research question or *hypothesis*   A best guess based on observation or research evidence, to be accepted or rejected on the basis of information gathered in a particular study.

Research setting   Situation where behavior is evaluated.

Reversibility   Ability to think about the logical consequences of retracing a line of reasoning back to its beginning.

Rooting reflex   The automatic response of infants when their cheek is stroked of turning their heads and sucking.

Sample   The group of subjects selected for study from the total population.

Self-concept   Awareness of how one is alike and different from other individuals. A positive self-concept is evidence that the individual rates well in his own estimation in comparison with other individuals.

Self-demand schedule   Arranging opportunity for feeding and sleeping according to the infant's observed need.

Self-esteem   The value an individual places on himself or herself.

Sensorimotor period   First stage in Piaget's theory covering the first two years of life. Learning at this stage takes place through the sense and manipulation of materials.

Separation anxiety   Emotional response of infant to separation from mother or caregiver.

Sex role concept   Behavior characteristic identified with one sex.

Sex-typed   Behavior and toys traditionally associated with either males or females.

Social class   Division of society into groups according to education, occupation, and income level of the head of the family.

Solitary play   Playing alone.

Stacking toys   Play materials that require placing one piece on top of the other, usually with a rod to hold the pieces together.

Statistical analysis   Techniques for numerical analysis to determine the probability that findings of the study can be explained on the basis of chance alone.

Stranger anxiety   Fear of strange persons or places.

Subjects   The specific children and/or adults selected for study.

Symbolic play   Use of imagination in labeling items and acting out familiar happenings.

Temper tantrum   Display and release of anger and frustration.

Title IV-A day care programs Comprehensive day care for poor children financed under Title IV-A of the Social Security Act.

Toddlerhood Age range from twelve to thirty months of age.

Trust First stage in Erikson's theory of personality development covering the first year of life.

Visual accommodation Automatic adjustment of the eye for seeing different distances.

WPA nursery schools First federal program for education of children under age six; sponsored by the Works Progress Administration during the Depression.

Index

Photo Credits

Cover, Jim Lynch

EFGHIJ–H–79